CLIMBING OUT
of the Pit
# of Life

by

DR DARREL HO-YEN

BMSc (Hons) MBChB MRCPath MD

DODONA BOOKS

ISBN 0-9511090-4-9

Published and distributed by
Dodona Books,
The Old Schoolhouse, Kirkhill,
Inverness IV5 7PE

**British Library Cataloguing in
Publication Data**
A catalogue record of this book is
available from the British Library.

Typeset by XL Publishing Services
Nairn, and printed in Great Britain
by Highland Printers, Inverness

CONTENTS

Case history. Comment. Major factors in coping(speed of events, emotional support, confidence, resilience, system of beliefs). The solution. Summary.

Tom. Observation. Case histories. Comment. The idea of a ladder. Rungs of the ladder (lifeless, anger, denial, disgrace, endeavour, renewal). The stages (order, intensity, time, other problems). Climbing out. Summary.

John. Observation. Case histories. Comment. Major factors (inactivity, physical needs, emotional needs). The solution : act, satisfy physical needs (food, drink, sleep), satisfy emotional needs (crying, touching) and enjoy yourself. Summary.

Irene and Rob. Observation. Case histories. Comment. Major factors (helpless, misdirected, repressed, with other negative emotions, appropriate). The solution : knowledge of anger and its combinations, preparation for provocation, dealing with confrontation, using blocking techniques (3 D's), getting rid of anger and avoiding rumination. Summary.

The Fifth Duke of Portland. Observation. Case histories.

Comment. Major factors (facts, feelings, others, reality). The Solution : knowledge, time and acceptance. Summary.

Gordon Bennett. Observation. Case histories. Comment. Major factors (facts, feelings, others, reality,). The solution : knowledge, time and acceptance. Summary.

Barnes Wallis. Observation. Case histories. Comment. Major factors (time, self, principles). The solution : personal and social. Summary.

Charles. Observation. Case histories. Comment. Major factors (dependence, replacements, the past). The solution : responsibility, living without and finding yourself. Summary.

The minister. Observation. Case histories. Comment. Major factors (wounded, fear). The solution : healing and growth. The next pit. Summary.

Dinner party. Observation. Major factors : definition of happiness, unhappiness, personal factors (outlook, age, sex and marriage, prosperity) and amount of happiness. The solution : personal life, relationships and environment. Conclusion. Summary.

4

ABOUT THE AUTHOR

Dr Darrel Ho-Yen was born in Guyana, South America, and finished his schooling in London. After a year's Voluntary Service Overseas in the Caribbean, he went to medical school at Dundee University. He completed his training at the Regional Virus Laboratory, Ruchill Hospital Glasgow. He is now Consultant Microbiologist at Raigmore Hospital NHS Trust, Inverness; Director of the Scottish Toxoplasma Reference Laboratory; and Honorary Clinical Senior Lecturer at Aberdeen University.

Dr Ho-Yen has had extensive experience in managing and counselling patients with Post Viral Fatigue Syndrome and the first edition of **Better Recovery from Viral Illnesses** (1985) was the first book on this subject (2nd ed 1987; 3rd ed 1993, reprinted 1994). He is also a co-author of the Oxford University Press textbook for medical students and postgraduate doctors **"Diseases of Infection"** (1987 and 1993).

His experience on the needs of patients with chronic illnesses prompted him to write "**Unwind! Understand and control life be better!!**" in 1991 (reprinted 1994). He was also joint editor of "**Human Toxoplasmosis**", a book for scientists and medical practitioners published by Oxford University Press in 1992. Dr Ho-Yen has published numerous scientific papers and articles for medical practitioners and the general public.

PREFACE

Over the years, I have been asked by many patients to write a book on how they may deal with a great loss. In my books, "Better Recovery From Viral Illnesses" and "Unwind", I had briefly mentioned some of the consequences of an individual's great loss. **However I have been asked to provide detailed descriptions of the emotional reactions to great loss and solutions on how they may be dealt with.**

Many books on great loss concentrate on bereavement, but many other great losses can be comparable in its effects on the individual. Also, the individual will have to go through similar stages as in bereavement to come to terms with his/her loss. **This book looks upon great loss as the pit of life, and the solutions to dealing with the loss as a ladder to climb out of the pit.**

No book is published by the efforts of only one person. I am grateful for the support of **Gregory and Colan** during the writing of this book. **Rob Polson** has been very helpful in getting scientific and other information for me. I am particularly grateful to **Alan Bowley** for his comments which were both devastating and instructive. **Jean Chatterton, David Ashburn and Roger Evans** were excellent at proof reading. **Grant Shipcott** of XL Publishing has been a tremendous help in producing the cover and typesetting the book. **Forbes Cunningham** of Highland Printers has been extremely cooperative.

Lastly, **Lorna Wycherley** has survived yet another book, and as always, she has demonstrated unbelievable understanding and stamina in preparing the numerous drafts of this book.

Dr Darrel O. Ho-Yen
April 1995

CHAPTER ONE

THE PIT OF LIFE

I see many patients who have to cope with disasters in their lives. The word "pit" best describes the situation where someone is walking along with few troubles when there is a sudden fall into a potentially disastrous situation. At one instant, the person is quite content and the next moment he/she is in darkness in a deep opening in the ground – a pit. The pit of life is a low point of an individual's existence. Suddenly, life is disrupted, turned upside down and the individual is helpless. **The pit may be many things : death of a loved one, the end of a relationship, severe illness, financial ruin, a severe accident, betrayal, public humiliation, loss of a job or an enforced change of life.**

Many of these major life crises are unpredictable. Yet, one needs to deal with the situation. Any one of them can be difficult, but when there are several crises at once, everything appears hopeless. **How can one deal with these crises and how difficult will it be?** First, I must say that I have not included in the pit changes that are a normal part of life and which most people do not have great difficulty in coping with (such as puberty, adolescence, courtship, pregnancy and menopause). Are the major crises which I have described as a pit comparable? One can say that a severe illness is usually not a result of one's behaviour, whereas one may have contributed to one's financial ruin or divorce. However, **this book is not intended to**

9

judge why something happened, but rather to concentrate on dealing with the problem when it has happened. Consider someone breaking a leg in a car accident, in some cases, the person's poor driving might be the cause; alternatively it could be completely the other driver's fault. But does apportioning the blame help the situation? The answer is no; wherever the fault, the victim still has to recover from a broken leg. **This book concentrates on the process of healing rather than on recrimination.**

Another factor is that some authorities look upon grief after bereavement as quite different from grief from other causes. Although I accept that there are significant differences, in my experience, it is a mistake not to recognise the considerable effects of the other crises that I have described as the pit. **My approach is one in which all of the crises of the pit are treated in a similar way, as a great loss. This book provides instruction on how to deal with great loss.**

CASE HISTORY

In 1984, Sharon M Carr was diagnosed as having a malignant brain tumour. To a teenager, this could have been so devastating that life would not have been worth living. Not so for Sharon. She, in a series of poems, documented her journey in coming to terms with her illness and herself. Her book of poems, **"Yet life was a triumph"** published by World (UK) Milton Keynes, 1992 (ISBN 0-85009-549-2), is a great tribute to her courage. In May 1989 she graduated from Emory University, United States of America. She was in a wheelchair and the Dean of the University brought the diploma down to where she sat. At lunch, she could not feed herself, but was happy and laughed with great gusto. Her poetry shows a quite extraordinary journey from bewilderment, grief, anger, peace and also has her epitaph (the titles of the poems are in brackets) :

a) Bewilderment :

"She didn't wipe the tear away. It fell weakly,
        like the crumpled leaf after torrential wind;
It carved a vermilion gutter into her face,
            burning, scorching, rending,
        the visage of assurance, until the true features
                    belched forth –
she never lifted a finger to hide her shame."
                        (She didn't wipe the tear)

"He has torn that he may heal us,
and we are stricken, but our faithful Lord
will bind us up."
                        (Torn, to be healed)

b) Grief :

"My friend was innocent. You killed him.
        Someday, you stupid sick stone,
my friend will salt His bread with the silt
            of your destruction."
                        (Death of a good friend)

"Don't you get tired of teaching me how to die,
how to grieve with patience for the unresolved,
how to tumble from the treetop…
Hard is the ground, the discipline of dirt in eyelashes,

11

the throbbing temple filled with cancer."

(Learning to die)

c) Anger

"A thousand tears have come and gone,
    and I am not yet empty,
The tide of foaming pain-laced sorrow
        has pommelled the sand of my refuge,
            yet I am not beaten."

(Count down)

"I prayed about promises,
        and wanting to feel protected about
        the ME they were threatening to take away;
I prayed about wills,
            and frustrating grief,
                and tension."

(Acceptance)

"I will be waiting for you
            in whatever tomorrow you awake to
            and we will embrace in light
            that is no longer fleeting."

(The mortality of lighting)

d) Peace :

"Miracles are so often silent,
        slinking into our hurried lives like leopards leaving
        the sanctum of animal power
        to lie down in a world of men."

(Jungle progeny)

"We try to bridge the gap
    between physical and spiritual, the mental
    and emotional,
    with claps of doctrine and learning until we
    remember
                bats are blind."
                        (The cave)

"A parasite destroys me,
    like the demon justice of the dark side
    of creation, cleansing while scrubbing."
                      (The solstice)

"Now I lay me down to sleep,
        not knowing if the climb to morning
            will prove too steep ..."
                (At the end of the day)

e) Epitaph :

"I am sustained by what I cannot see,
        and reassured by a comforting grasp
        that is all in all, ever powerful, ever good."
                      (Epitaph)
"death is tender,
        and life was a triumph."
                      (Epitaph)

COMMENT

Sharon Carr was a very unusual person. Nevertheless,
**when normal individuals are faced with great loss,
they are forced to behave in an unusual way.** For

most with time and support, they are eventually able to recover from their loss; for a minority, the events are so traumatic that there is no recovery from this situation. What would you do? How would you deal with great loss?

After a great loss, one experiences intense emotions. Sharon's poetry describes the "shame" and being "torn"; followed by being "innocent" in the situation with a "throbbing temple filled with cancer". Yet, her "frustrating grief" becomes "death is tender". **These complicated, mixed emotions are all part of the process of dealing with great loss.** This book will provide you with information on the stages you will go through in dealing with a great loss.

MAJOR FACTORS IN COPING

In any situation, some individuals are able to cope easily whilst others struggle. These different responses are exaggerated when one is considering major life crises. The explanation for many is that the ability to deal with major problems is a matter of luck. I believe that this approach is like the old saying : **"Good luck is a lazy man's estimate of a worker's success."** In reality, a person's ability to cope with major life crises is mostly dependent on recognized factors. One can easily give the likelihood of any individual's ability to cope. **The main factors are :**

1. **Speed of Events** : If a crisis is sudden and totally unexpected, it usually makes it more difficult for someone to understand and cope. Whereas if a crisis

was anticipated, especially if over many months, then obviously the process of coping would have been started before the actual event. Although it is easy to understand this in relation to accidents, it also applies to other losses. A particularly difficult situation can be coping with sudden unemployment, especially if one expected to be working for another twenty-five years.

2. **Emotional Support** : If one is isolated and without any emotional support, life is difficult even without a major life crisis. Obviously, it is much easier for those with an extensive network of good friends and relatives to cope with crises and disasters as there are many to share the burden. This allows help with the day to day problems of living, such as shopping and paying bills. However, it is the emotional support that is the most valuable. Those with a loss also need the social reassurance that their situation is appreciated.

3. **Confidence** : Confidence must not be underestimated. It is said that : "The difference between the possible and the impossible is in the mind of man." Time and time again throughout life, one sees two people with equal abilities, but the person with confidence succeeds whilst the other fails. Confidence is a tremendous asset and this is accentuated when there is a crisis. The reason is that with great loss, there is usually under-performance and those with confidence can be apparently less affected as they are starting from a higher level.

4. **Resilience** : China usually breaks when it falls to the ground; rubber bounces. The effects of a crisis on any one individual are similar. For some, it is too much and

15

they dissolve into an emotional mess; but for others it is only another event to survive. The ability to absorb shocks, as though one was made of rubber, is a great asset. This does not mean one must not show any emotion, but rather that one should still be able to carry on with day to day living. Obviously it is appropriate to show emotion over a loss, however combined with resilience the emotion does not become overwhelming.

5. **System of Beliefs** : A system of beliefs can provide exceptional emotional support, also there is usually some preparation for adversity. This must not be trivialised. For someone blind, there can be great strength in :

"We walk by faith, not by sight."

(Corinthians 2, 5 v7.)

For someone without beliefs, there can be difficulty in explaining, understanding and reconciling many of life's more difficult situations. It is a great comfort if one can believe that what has happened was part of God's plan. Alternatively, if one believed that life is simply a matter of how the cards were dealt, losses are expected. The vulnerable situation is where one feels that there is no meaning or pattern to life.

THE SOLUTION

You cannot avoid the pit of life. It is a part of your existence, but there is usually no preparation for dealing with the pit. In the last century, it was felt that you would "instinctively" have all the required knowledge of sex. This is now known to be incorrect and there is great

16

emphasis on sex education in schools. **Today the pit of life is a similar situation where there is expectation that somehow you will know what you have to do to climb out.** Reality is different. As with sex, to perform well you require sufficient knowledge to know what to do. You need to have information. **This book will explain the stages you will go through after great loss and suggest what you should do.**

SUMMARY

1. The pit of life is a low point of your existence. It is usually unexpected and you are initially turned upside down and helpless.

2. The pit may have many causes : death of a loved one, the end of a relationship, severe illness, financial ruin, a severe accident, betrayal, public humiliation, loss of a job or an enforced change of life.

3. It is possible, as Sharon Carr has shown, to climb out of the pit and make life a triumph. Great strength is required.

4. Your ability to recover from a major life crisis is influenced by : speed of events, emotional support, confidence, resilience and retention of a system of beliefs.

5. It is easier to climb out of the pit if you are aware of the stages you will go through after a great loss and know what you should do in each stage.

CHAPTER TWO

THE LADDER

Tom had just graduated with a degree in law and his future seemed bright. Nevertheless, he needed reassurance and so went to a fortune-teller. She was expensive because of her world-wide fame, and as she gazed into her crystal ball, she said :

"Your future is extraordinarily good. You will be a great success."

Tom beamed. He had always wanted to be a lawyer and this was justification of his dedication and hard work over many years. But he wanted to learn more and so said :

"Good. I guess that my honours degree and good testimonials mean that I shall easily get a good job."

The fortune-teller looked into her crystal ball again and then replied :

"Yes. You will get a wonderful job. There will be 200 applicants for the job, but you will get the job."

Tom was delighted. Things were really going well; he was over-joyed. He added :

"My dad is also top of his profession and as I will be in the same profession, he can help me."

Again, the fortune-teller's answer was reassuring.

"Yes. Your father will play a major part in your future success."

Tom could not control himself any longer and blurted out:

"Yes! Yes! I know all of this. I guess that with all that you have told me, am I already near the top of the ladder?"

This obvious question was met with a bewildered stare by the fortune-teller who replied :

"Oh no! You have misunderstood. Your future is bright, of that there is no doubt. But what stands between you and the top of the ladder is the ladder."

-o-0-o-

Observation

It is so very easy for each of us to over-estimate our position. We can feel that by right we should be half way up or near the top of the ladder. **As for Tom, someone had to tell him that he had not started to climb the ladder. When life is difficult we need to be more realistic than ever, and we need to know where we are.** Those around us can often be of help by telling us how far we have to go. Sadly, we often believe that we know best! How can anyone else appreciate how complex and intricate our situation is, or, how good we are at dealing with crises? **The truth is devastating : our situation is often complex only to us. For others, our situation is quite straightforward and simple.** Also, as we think our problem is complex, obvious answers may elude us whilst to others there is no real difficulty. When we can recognize that there are simple answers, we can get on and do the work of climbing the ladder, rather than feel there are no answers to our complex problem.

CASE HISTORIES

CASE ONE

Elizabeth was a 30 year old with two children aged 8 and 10 years. She was a successful hairdresser because of her obvious ability and likeable personality. Her husband was a company director with a good income. Her family lived a mile away, were supportive and she was an active member of the local community. The family were happy. Then disaster struck. Her husband, returning from a business trip, was killed in a road traffic accident. The effects on Elizabeth were dramatic. She was totally lifeless, walking around in a daze and obviously shocked. Arrangements had to be made for the children and herself, and she was totally incapable of making the simplest decision. She stayed off work, weeks passed without her taking a bath, bills were not paid and the children ran riot. Eventually, family and friends took over. They cooked meals, looked after the kids and arranged for the household chores to be done.

Two months passed, but Elizabeth remained in a state of shock. She kept being angry that her husband was dead and so could not deal with her problems. Her emotions were volatile and she seemed always to be crying as she watched any television programme. Her doctor and parents became more and more worried. Her previous confidence appeared to have deserted her. She stopped going to church as she blamed God for her husband's death. Then a letter arrived from her husband's barber. He first apologised for his not having written before, but went on to say how he had enjoyed her husband's visits. Apparently, her husband had frequently talked of her and had always said that she was the rock of their marriage. The barber went on to give detailed descriptions of her behaviour as seen by her husband. She read the letter ten times. When she put down the letter, she had a long bath and washed her hair. The next day she started behaving as her husband had described to the barber. A month later, she was coping with her family on her own, and two months later she returned to work.

CASE TWO

Lorna was a 26 year old secretary with a 6 year old daughter. She had returned home one day to find that her husband had left her to live with the 18 year old babysitter. Her situation appeared disastrous : money was tight, her parents were dead, her job was difficult and she did not have any religious beliefs. She sat down and poured herself a large gin. Then, she stroked the cat. After an hour, she got up and fed her daughter before putting her to bed. Afterwards, she returned to the sitting room and poured herself another drink. She drank, looked into space, stroked the cat and started to think.

Time went quickly as there was so much to think about : Why had she got married? What had he done for her? What did she want and what did she want for her daughter? She sat on her chair for the entire night; she finished the bottle of gin but was never drunk. Fortunately the next day was Saturday. She left her daughter with a friend at 9.00 am and returned home and went to bed. She slept for 10 hours, picked up her daughter and gave her a great, big cuddle. She returned to work on Monday determined to cope. Two months later, she found herself in a better job with no financial problems, her daughter was happy and she was enjoying her independence.

COMMENT

Both of these case histories have a common start : the woman being suddenly left alone. With Case One, there was considerable outside support and one might have expected that she might have coped with great ease, but she did not. With Case Two, there was little outside support and one might have predicted that she would have problems in coping. **This is the difficulty with statistics : they can say who might or might not have difficulties, but it may not be applicable to any one individual's situation.** Yet, both of these women did eventually cope. How was this achieved? Was the process different for each? How would you and I cope? Quite amazingly, the process of coping with disasters is similar despite the disaster or the support any individual has. **This book carefully describes each stage of the process of coping with disasters.** This information will allow you to be more aware, more knowledgeable and to cope better with adversity in life.

THE IDEA OF A LADDER

The use of the ladder is the easiest way to get out of the pit of life. Many people simply believe that **"time heals."** This is true, but how does time heal? It heals in many people by allowing them to go through the process of the ladder. Thus **the ladder is the process by which time**

heals the suffering of the individual. Like much of what we do in life, it can be instinctive. We muddle on, glad to be able to get through each day. This is totally understandable in a desperate situation. Indeed, it seems rather excessive to ask people in a crisis to think. There is no time or desire to think. However, **whenever we cannot find time to think the job often takes ten times as long to do.** Thus knowledge of the ladder allows the individual to solve his/her problem sooner. **Less time is wasted in the slow process of trial and error and allowing the effects of the pit to be overshadowed by other newer experiences.**

The ladder is nothing mystical. It is simply the result of observing many patients going through crises. **The ladder is a result of my conclusions on the best way for patients to deal with their personal disasters.** I have always been impressed by how some individuals recover quickly and others take a lifetime. Yet, both seem to be putting in the same amount of time and energy. After many years, it became obvious what was the main difference between the two groups of patients. Those who made no progress spent their time and energy walking around the bottom of the pit, contemplating climbing the ladder. **Those who made a fast recovery were able to methodically use their time and energy to climb the ladder.**

Quite simply, one group got on with the business of recovery; whilst the other group just thought about it. Case One should have recovered faster than Case Two, but she did not. The reason was that Case Two used the ladder to climb out of the pit. Over the years, I have seen many patients who appeared not to have a good chance of recovery, but who were able to surprise me. **As a result, I have devised the ladder to describe the stages everyone goes through after a major crisis.** In other books, these stages have also been mentioned but often not in great detail. I have created the "ladder" to give the reader greater information and a sense of where you are. It also allows the patient to easily remember the different stages of recovery. **The ladder is like the key which can open the lock. Once the door is open, the knowledge allows rapid recovery as one can see one's situation as a process of adjusting to a great loss.**

RUNGS OF THE LADDER

The ladder contains the fundamental insight on which this book is based. When one is in a disastrous situation and needs help, the ladder provides this help. **The rungs of the ladder are the first letters of the stages that are necessary for you to go through to recover.** There are seven stages :-

1. **Lifeless** : shocked and lost. One feels dead. There is no emotion. One cannot think. Numbness is everywhere. Physical needs disappear. Nothing matters. Death would be a welcome release.
2. **Anger** : Why should this happen to me? There is anger about the unfairness of it all. The betrayal. There is no recognition of one's great efforts. Life is bitter. Vengeance is not enough. One is on the ground and there is a queue of people who want to take advantage of the situation.
3. **Denial** : One denies that the situation has happened.

There is disbelief. It could not happen to me. It is a mistake. It is all wrong. There is also a yearning and searching for the previous life. There is a great need to imagine everything right, whatever the cost. There is an imposed exile from the community.

4. **Disgrace** : One's failure is public. One's social status and identity have changed. The community reflects on one's loss. There is isolation as the community deliberates. There can be a loss of faith. Values disappear : alcohol and pills appear attractive if only to relieve the pain.

5. **Endeavour** : This stage is masked by action, by striving and by effort to deal with the loss. It is when one starts to see one's situation more precisely. The truth is faced. There is acceptance of reality. There are no half-measures but the cold truth is addressed. This is the turning point.

6. **Renewal** : This is the new dawn when all is renewed – given new vigour. The individual is able to reflect on the past and starts to heal, and build for the future. There is consolidation and growth : a new person emerges, richer for the experience, wiser and stronger.

THE STAGES

The stages in the ladder as described above are in the order that most patients experience them. However there are several important aspects of the ladder to remember:

a) **order** : For any one patient, the order may be different although all of the stages may be experi-

25

enced. This is because the order is influenced by circumstances and an individual's personality. Thus for a public figure, disgrace may be one of the first emotions experienced. Similarly, for someone in whom anger is rare, this may be a minor emotion. There may also be regression to an earlier stage of the ladder.

b) **intensity** : The various stages in the ladder do not have the same effect. For some, the first stage (lifeless) is extremely intense and overpowering – the patient is in total shock; whereas denial may be a minor factor, accompanied by weak, transient emotions. Again circumstances may dictate that a particular stage is very intense, for example disgrace in a bankruptcy.

c) **time** : The time spent in each stage can vary considerably. Thus Case One spent two months in the first stage, but then quickly passed through the remaining five stages in an equal period. Case Two spent very little time in stage one, and completed the entire process in two months. Again the time spent in each stage is dependent on circumstances and an individual's personality.

d) **other problems** : The stages may also be influenced by other problems in a patient's life. Financial problems are particularly important here. If there is a sudden great need to earn money, this can be overwhelming and the main concern. Similarly, the need to care for children can be a major preoccupation. Other problems can have one of two effects; they may prevent progression through the stages of the ladder as the individual is preoccupied; alternatively, they may help to accelerate progression through the stages of the ladder.

CLIMBING OUT

It is comforting to recognize the stages of the ladder are predictable and a necessary process for someone dealing with a great loss. However, this knowledge merely identifies the problem, but does not provide any solutions. Matters can be further complicated as someone may not want to climb out of the pit of life. A few individuals are so traumatised by their loss that they can choose to remain lifeless or angry for the rest of their lives. This does not apply to most. For the majority, the problem of climbing out of the pit is that they do not know how to do it. This book emphasizes that the ladder is the key, but just as important, **detailed solutions are provided on how someone may progress from one rung of the ladder to another.** Anyone may choose to stay in the pit, but one should not remain there longer than is necessary through ignorance.

SUMMARY

1. When life is difficult we need to be more realistic than ever, and we need to know where we are.

2. We tend to think of our situation as complex and intricate when it can appear quite straightforward and simple to others.

3. The process of coping with all disasters is similar despite the differences in the causes or the support any individual has. The individual who looks least likely to succeed has the ability to surprise.

4. The ladder is the process by which time heals the suffering of the individual. It is a result of observing many patients dealing with their crises.

5. The ladder describes the stages everyone goes through after a major crisis. Knowledge of this process can save a lot of time and suffering.

6. The ladder stands for : **l**ifeless, **a**nger, **d**enial, **d**isgrace, **e**ndeavour and **r**enewal.

7. Although the stages are described in the order most patients experience, there are considerable variations in the order, intensity of emotions and duration of each stage or when other problems are present.

8. Variations are influenced by an individual's circum-stances and personality; these may both delay or accelerate progression through the stages.

9. This book provides detailed solutions on how to progress from one rung of the ladder to another. This knowledge equips the climber to emerge from the pit of life by the quickest route.

CHAPTER THREE
LIFELESS

The country had not seen such floods, cars were buried and even houses had only their roofs above water. The toll on livestock was enormous. John, an old farmer, was looking at his water covered land with disbelief. Just then, his neighbour drove up in his Range Rover, and said :

"I'm sorry John. Your sheep were all washed down the river."

John stood silent and softly asked :

"What about Lawson's sheep?"

"They're gone too" was the reply.

"And Fitzgerald's sheep?"

"Gone too. Everyone has lost their sheep."

"Humph!!" responded John, immediately cheering up with the news.

"It isn't as bad as I thought!"

-o-O-o-

Observation

The first rung of the ladder is "Lifeless." This is the stage when we feel that life is not worth living. Everything is against us, and it is easier to curl up in the corner and die. All around us is devastation and you feel shocked, without hope and there seems no future. **We are without life – *lifeless*.** Then, something happens, you see some shared experiences, some good, a noble

29

action, a smile, some concern and it is enough. Enough for the fire of life to be nurtured back into a full flame. For John, it was simply that his neighbours were in the same situation and he was not alone. **This chapter is about raking over the ashes of a fire that appears dead, and finding a few glowing embers that can be fanned into a flame.**

CASE HISTORIES

CASE ONE

Bill was a whizz-kid who could do anything with computers. During the 1980's, he was in great demand. At 28 years he had his own business, a large salary, a BMW car and an attractive wife. Life was good but he had earned it and still worked 16 hour days. But time moved on and the 1990's were not good years. The recession hit his business, and he had to take a large salary cut. His customers refused to pay, the bank called in his loans and he was made bankrupt.

Suddenly his world ended. He did not have to work; he stayed at home and sat watching the world go by. He felt that there was a great divide between himself and the rest of the world. There was an invisible wall and he did not belong to the community on the other side. They were in a different world from which he was now excluded because of his financial position. Across the wall, there was the real life with great enjoyment, emotion and vitality. On his side of the wall, there was just great emptiness without feelings. In the game of life, he had been given some good cards and now it was his turn to have some bad cards, after which the game would finish. Bill kept playing these bad cards for weeks. Then one sunny day, Bill decided to go and buy a newspaper. As he was about to cross the road, he saw an old lady with a white stick who appeared to be bewildered by the noise of the traffic. He went over to the old lady and helped her across the road. She was immensely grateful and put her hand on his and said : "Bless you!" As he watched the old lady walk down the street, he felt great admiration and respect for her courage despite her disabilities. He felt ashamed and stood still and cried. Afterwards, he felt relief. He went and bought his newspaper, but he also bought a chocolate ice-cream. As he walked home eating his ice-cream in the sunshine, he felt the happiness of his youth. There was much he had to be grateful for and in the past he was just too busy to enjoy the simple pleasures of life.

CASE TWO

Derek was destroyed. A freak accident at his work had resulted in his losing both of his legs. He was a keen rugby player with some talent who would now be able to watch only from the side-lines. Life was unfair and he felt that he did not want to live. He was lifeless. He spent all day watching television, but he did not see. Everything was make-believe; there was no reality. Everyone around him, and he himself, were simply actors in a terrible soap drama. He almost felt that after the commercial break, he would be able to screw his legs back on again. Even when he had been discharged from hospital and his legs had healed, he felt he was not well enough to be at home. He was a child again, and there

31

was so much that he could not do for himself. He resented the stumps that he had for legs, even though they had healed perfectly. When he saw his legs, he could see only loss.

Then, one day as he sat in his wheelchair on the lawn, the neighbour's dog came up to him. Derek was no animal lover and was about to shoo the dog away. But the dog just came up to him and sat. Despite his reservations, Derek found himself stroking the dog. The dog licked his hand and then licked the stumps of his legs with simple affection. Derek looked, felt the coldness of the dog's licks and wept. The dog immediately sat down, confused by his crying. Eventually, Derek raised his hand and patted the dog who wagged his tail furiously in response. For the rest of the day, Derek and the dog played. They shared his lunch and Derrick cried and laughed more than he had in the previous three months. At the end of the day, Derek held the dog in his arms tightly, nuzzled the dog and kissed it.

COMMENT

Both of these cases had quite different problems to deal with : financial ruin in Case One and a physical disability in Case Two. Yet, the way that both of these men responded to their crises was remarkably similar. They were at the first stage of the ladder – **lifeless**. Then something happened which allowed them to proceed to the next stage. This "something" could be interpreted as chance, and in many ways this is how "time heals." **If you give yourself enough time, something will happen that will allow you to progress. However this**

is very wasteful of time. It is also possible to understand your situation, and use knowledge of what is happening to you to progress. Knowledge is neither "mystical", "chance", "luck", or "good fortune". It can be obvious, predictable and used to your advantage. It is said : "Those who have most knowledge have most luck".

This chapter is aimed at providing knowledge to you so that you will not need to depend on chance or luck, and so that you will not need to rely on time creating the right circumstances for your progress. **Instead you will have the knowledge to make faster progress, to be lucky and have good fortune.**

MAJOR FACTORS

After a great loss, one is shocked and numbed. **The body needs time to cope with the loss and as it tries to adjust, it does nothing.** The characteristics of this stage are similar to the medical condition of shock in which there is apparent inactivity with no real physical or emotional needs. For those around the individual this stage can be worrying, especially as it may last many weeks. Major factors are :

1. **Inactivity** : The individual appears to be in a permanent dream. It is not uncommon for someone to sit in a darkened room for hours, or stand looking out the window but not notice what is happening. The person's thoughts are permanently elsewhere. Questions are met with a staring dazed look and everything has to be repeated many times. The answers are always, "No, thank you" or "I'm all right."

Previous hobbies or favourite television programmes produce no interest. The person has become totally different – lifeless.

2. **Physical Needs** : Appetite suddenly disappears and it is difficult to persuade the person to eat, even a favourite food. Even favourite foods such as chocolate and ice-cream are not temptations. Equally, there is little desire to drink. Often a cup of tea would go cold without the individual having taken a single sip. Favourite drinks appear to have as much appeal as cod liver oil. Sleep becomes difficult with nightmares and vivid dreams. Sound sleep of 1-2 hours would be followed by tossing and turning for the rest of the night.

3. **Emotional Needs** : The person hides from the rest of the world, preoccupied by the great loss. Friends and relatives are avoided. Meals are taken early so as not to meet others in the canteen. Routines such as shopping are changed so that no one recognizes the person. Curtains are drawn and lights switched off so that there is no temptation for visitors to ring the door bell. If there is a chance meeting, it is quickly terminated by "Hi! Good to see you. Must hurry" or "Hello! I'm in a rush to get to the dentist. Must see you soon".

THE SOLUTION

The object is to move from the position of feeling lifeless to living life again. This is the first rung in the ladder and in many ways it is the most difficult. Once you have started on the journey, you are carried along by momentum. **But at the beginning, there needs to be**

great resolve and will just to get started. The seasons of the year are a good example of the opposites if life being part of the natural process : the hotness of summer will eventually be replaced by the winter. However, there are also more subtle balances in life. There is the wisecrack:

"For every woman who makes a fool of some man, there is another who makes a man of some fool."

There are a few simple things you can do to move away from a lifeless state to the next rung in the ladder. **At a time when you have very little motivation and there is a great need to watch the world pass by, positive action needs to be taken.** The important decisions are to :

1. **Act** : To act is to affirm life and to deny being lifeless. The Scottish poet Robert Burns, put this truth very simply :

   "Let us do or die".

   It does not matter what you do. It can be knitting, sewing, redecorating the bedroom or any mundane, repetitive task. **The essence is that there is a product of your efforts – you have made a mark so you are not lifeless.** Simple jobs around the house are probably best as there are many and they are usually of a repetitive nature. For some individuals, there is a need to do something creative – write a poem, paint a picture, or do flower arranging. **It does not matter what you do, as long as there is a recognizable product for your hours of labour.**

2. **Satisfy physical needs** : The body will die unless its physical needs are satisfied. Leo Tolstoy said it very clearly : "Our body is a machine for living. It is

organised for that, it is its nature". **A machine requires to be serviced and the requirements of your body are :**

a) **food** : You need to eat sufficiently to sustain life. Many have lost kilograms of weight going through the stages of the ladder. This can be beneficial if you are overweight, but if you are not, eat to live.

b) **drink** : It is easy to stop drinking, to get dehydrated and then to have to deal with health problems (such as urinary tract infections). Try to enjoy your drinks. Go to the supermarket and pretend you are a child, again get the "Cremola Foam" – act crazy!!

c) **sleep** : Cervantes said "Sleep is the best cure for waking troubles". For most, sleep is a real problem as it becomes disturbed, fitful and accompanied by unpleasant dreams. Yet it is important to get enough sleep as sleep can cure. If necessary take a large brandy at night or get sleeping tablets from your doctor. Alternatively, be creative. Go for a five mile jog, follow this with a long bath and then hot drinking chocolate.

3. **Satisfy Emotional Needs** : In a crisis, your feelings are heightened and intensified. Yet, many feel that they should subjugate these strong emotions. They remember a generation ago when it was said : "Men do not cry" or "adults must be strong". The truth is quite different. **Crying and emotions depend on the situation : if you are in a disaster, the only adult response may be to cry.** Being a man or adult is

therefore about behaving in a way appropriate to the situation. There are two important factors.

a) **Crying** : Perhaps more than any other emotion, crying is a great release. It is the first way that you have learnt to express yourself – Your first noises in this world, at birth, were those of a cry. It is appropriate as you go through great anguish that you should express yourself in this way. It can be a great mistake to resist crying.

b) **Touching** : Touching is one of our most gratifying forms of communication. A pat on the hand or shoulder can say more than a thousand words. Yet, during a crisis, many try and withdraw and avoid other people, especially touching them. The converse is more appropriate, you should react to a crisis by going up to your friends and holding onto them, squeezing and hugging them. The warmth and benefit of such actions are worth more than several bottles of pills.

4. **Enjoy Yourself** : The ability to enjoy yourself is a triumph of life. It not only affirms that you are alive, but also loudly states that you are having fun. I once asked my son to write a diary about his holiday. He surprised me by writing at the end of each day "and we had fun". Children have a wonderful capacity to enjoy themselves despite the circumstances. Sometimes, it seems that adults take themselves too seriously and refuse to enjoy themselves unless everything else in their lives is good. Every day we have the ability to be content and it must be a crime to waste these opportunities. By enjoying yourself, I do not mean you have to have wild parties or go on a

world cruise. **I am speaking of simple enjoyment.** I am thinking of the joy of an ice-cream, a sausage roll, a perfect flower, the antics of the cat, the smell of the forest or the hope of sunrise. These are gifts that are meant to be enjoyed; they will give you fun and can make you content.

SUMMARY

1. The first stage of the ladder is being **lifeless.** Many depend on time, luck or chance to progress to the next stage.

2. Knowledge of how to progress to the next stage will save you much time. Less time will be spent in the slow process of trial and error.

3. To leave the stage of being lifeless, you must start to behave as though you are alive. You need to act and produce a recognizable product for your hours of labour.

4. You need to satisfy your physical needs : to have sufficient food, drink and sleep. Sleep in particular can be curative.

5. You need to satisfy your emotional needs : to cry and to touch. There is great benefit in being close to your friends.

6. The greatest affirmation of life is to enjoy yourself. Do not avoid enjoyment because of your situation, instead have fun and be content.

CHAPTER FOUR

ANGER

Irene and Rob were always angry and fighting. Their marriage was held together simply because their company needed both of them to survive. It was not financially possible for either to leave so they stayed together, but shouted and yelled at each other all day. The employees were always embarrassed and disturbed by these public quarrels.

One day, a young employee approached Rob and asked :

"I know that this is asking a lot, but I live at home with my parents. Tonight is my night for locking up the building. Do you mind if I bring my girlfriend back to the office later on tonight?"

Rob was taken aback but slowly replied :

"Why do you want to bring her back here? When I was your age I always took Irene to secluded places so that we could be alone."

The reply was swift :

"Oh, I don't mind being alone with my girlfriend, but I want to see her and for her to see me in a place that is well lit."

Rob was totally confused :

"Well lit? What do you want lights for? It is a lot easier when no one sees what you are doing."

His employee's reply was quick :

"It may be a lot easier without lights, but look at what happened to you. You and your wife are always angry with each other. It may have been better if you both could see what you were each like from the start!"

-o-0-o-

Observation

Anger is a strong emotion which can ruin lives. Rob's employee saw this and felt he should take steps to avoid such a situation. To some readers, it may be surprising that anger should be the next step after being lifeless. The explanation is as follows : as you return to life, you start to recognise your loss, and when you truly see how much you have lost you get angry. Anger is the expression of the loss (which may be in any of the crises that put you in the pit of life). Sometimes the anger is so great that it produces rage. Rage is worse than anger in that it is not possible to think properly, and a person may regress with a return to the lifeless stage. **More commonly, there is just the anger at the loss, the unfairness of it all and the need to blame somebody**. Anger is such a powerful emotion that it can be difficult to control, and it is possible for some to remain angry and bitter for the rest of their lives. Nevertheless, most people manage to progress to the next stage by understanding their anger.

CASE HISTORIES

CASE ONE

Denise was a teacher who appeared to have everything to live for. She was a single parent with two sons aged 6 and 7 years, but she managed to cope with a full time

40

job. In addition she was a marathon runner of some distinction. Then, at 35 years after a short illness, she was diagnosed as having multiple sclerosis. She was absolutely devastated and could not come to terms with her illness. When she was discharged from hospital, she quickly returned to work, determined to fight the illness.

The staff and pupils at school noticed a great change in her. She had a short temper and seemed to be always shouting. She appeared angry with everyone : at the pupils because they had their lives ahead of them; and at the staff because they did not have her problems. She blamed God for her situation and boycotted the school service. Any mention of the church was like a red rag to a bull, and everyone feared her anger. She was no better at home, in fact, she was worse. The children became afraid of her temper and she had even started to hit the two boys. But her worst behaviour she kept for herself. She despised herself for allowing herself to become ill, and sometimes would dig the fingernails of her right hand into her left forearm until there were five little pools of blood.

Then one day as she sat watching television, there was a programme on abandoned Romanian babies who had become infected with the human immunodeficiency virus. Their lives were hopeless and their living conditions were squalid. She looked and she saw their plight. After the programme was over, she sat and thought. An hour later, she called her sons. They came into the room expecting the worst, instead, they saw their mother on the floor pretending to be a horse, asking them if they would like a ride. For an hour, Denise and her sons played on the carpet. They laughed until their sides hurt, then they all had masses of chocolate and cake. Finally, she held them and said that everything would be all right.

CASE TWO

Sam was managing director of a firm that sold do-it-yourself equipment. He was a superb salesman who always managed to make his customers feel special. He enjoyed his work and his social life; he knew everyone and everyone knew him. He was respected and looked upon as a valuable member of the community. Then one day he came to work to find that his office was locked. He was told to go to the Board room where a young executive explained that his undoubted talents were not consistent with the firm's philosophy. Quite simply, the firm had been taken over, Sam was not needed, he was too old, his experience was inappropriate and he had ten minutes to empty his desk.

Sam was numbed. But he left the office with his head held high. He went home, took his best golf club into the back garden and hit the apple tree with such force that the club broke in two. He was angry, furiously so. How could management behave in this way? He was angry at the young executive with the smug smile; he was angry with the society that these individuals represented. His anger moved from management to the whole political system in the country. All was short-sighted and doomed to failure. The whole country was going downwards and real values were being lost.

Sadly, Sam's friends quickly got tired of his outbursts. Soon, this man who had been popular for 35 years of his working life was alone and isolated, propping up the bar.

One evening in his alcoholic haze, Sam saw the evening news in which there was the story of a pensioner defending his property against vandals. Suddenly, there was a flash of insight : this was a man fighting the system to preserve his own rights. Sam walked out of the public house. He bought a big bunch of flowers and surprised his wife by his early return from the public house. As he gave her the flowers, he put the first two fingers of his right hand in the form of a gun and motioned to shoot himself in the temple. Then he winked.

COMMENT

Both of these cases were individuals who had progressed from being lifeless to being angry. And they were angry! They also needed someone to blame and Case One blamed all the people around her, whilst Case Two blamed the system. They were both helpless in their anger, and could have remained in this stage for a long time. Instead, **both managed to lose their anger and to progress to the next rung in the ladder.** How did they do this? Would you know what to do? Or would you be tempted to try and solve your problems with pills and alcohol?

MAJOR FACTORS

Anger is a feeling of great annoyance. It has no particular objective and often serves no useful purpose. Yet, after a loss, it is a very important emotional reaction. Sometimes it cannot be avoided and can take over one's life. Anger can be expressed in three ways : verbally, with shouting, screaming or abuse; physically by hitting, kicking or damaging property; and by turning inwards, suppressing the anger, having nightmares, ill-health and turning to alcohol and drugs. **Anger is therefore complex but there are five main types :**

1. **Helpless** : Here the individual's anger is a result of not being able to control the situation. The train is late; someone runs into your car whilst you are parked; someone dies; your house burns down. As the individual can do nothing, there is great agitation and tears. **There is a need to regain the ability to influence matters.**

2. **Misdirected** : This is the classic situation of blaming the messenger because the message is disliked. The person who sent the message is not there and so the messenger is attacked. There is a need to find a scapegoat. A relative dies so the hospital staff are blamed. The postman is shouted at because he delivers the speeding fine. Alternatively, it may be more complicated with the husband shouting at the wife's cooking when he really just wants to ask for some support. **There is a need to find the right target for the anger.**

3. **Repressed** : This is often not recognised as anger because the individual has repressed his/her true feelings. They had been brought up "not to scream" or "throw things". Instead, the anger is bottled up and results in poor health such as nightmares, headaches, tummy aches (even ulcers) or skin problems. **This anger can have serious long term consequences and must be recognised.**

4. **With Other Negative Emotions** : Anger is a frequent companion of other negative emotions. It is usually the weaker partner, but nevertheless its contribution can be significant :

- grief and anger, probably the commonest combination in bereavement
- fear and anger, especially when one is bullied or being taken advantage of
- sadness and anger, such as in the emotional separation of children from their parents
- depression and anger, probably the most common combination of all.

In all of these situations, the presence of anger may not receive consideration. Yet, anger is an important factor. With recognition, anger can be carefully dealt with and a positive outcome obtained.

5. **Appropriate** : Of all the types of anger, this is the most positive. It can be used to deal with the situation and obtain a good result. It is anger that is appropriate to the situation. Thus, if a child has been run down on a busy road, the community can direct its anger at obtaining a pedestrian crossing. Similarly, victims of any calamity can set up their own help-line or self-help group. **To progress up the ladder from the pit of life, you need this type of anger which turns a disastrous situation into one of benefit.**

The five types of anger do not necessarily exist alone. One can have several combinations, and worse one can have one combination which is replaced by another, different combination. **There are very, very many possible combinations of the five types of anger.** It is a bit like the national lottery, however, those with the most combinations do *not* stand the best chance of winning a great prize.

THE SOLUTION

The ability to turn anger into a useful product is a great asset. Although most individuals do not even consider that this is a possibility, it is more than just possible; for those with the knowledge, anger can be a useful tool in life rather than a great hindrance. **There are six stages in dealing with anger :**

1. **Knowledge of Anger and Its Combinations** : Most people look upon anger and other emotions, such as love, as similar : these emotions happen either by chance, luck or are God-given. They do not recognize that these emotions follow simple principles. It is much like learning your multiplication tables. The first stage is to have knowledge of what major type of anger you have (either helpless, misdirected, suppressed, with other negative emotions or appropriate – as in the last section of this book). Next, consider if you perhaps have a combination of several types of anger. Once you know what sort of anger you have, you have the knowledge to use it to your own benefit.

2. **Preparation for Provocation** : Anger is provoked by something, either a person or event. Once you are aware of the type(s) of anger relevant to your situation, it is then possible to predict the sort of situations that are likely to cause you anger. Thus, if you

have just been made unemployed, individuals in employment or references to your previous employer are likely to provoke anger. **With your knowledge, you can prepare yourself for such a provocation and work out how you will deal with it.** This may be reinforced by saying to yourself such as: "I can deal with this situation", "I can control my anger" or "I will not be provoked!"

3. **Dealing with Confrontation** : When the situation arises, the preparation that you have made will be tested. It is important not to avoid confrontation as then you cannot learn. You need to remember that it is a learning process so that with each confrontation you get better and better. It is a mistake to expect that you will be expert just because you have thought about it. You will be better than if you did not think, but expertise is only gained through much effort and failure. Make statements to yourself such as : "I know what is happening", "I am not afraid of this situation and I will not get angry", "I will learn from this experience" or "I must look after myself".

4. **Using Blocking Techniques** : These are the techniques by which you cope with the situation before anger develops. Your knowledge will allow you to block the cascade of events leading to anger. **The techniques are the 3 D's :**

   a) **deep breathing**. Half a dozen deep breaths taken in quick succession steady the nerves and focus your attention. Many performers and athletes use this technique before going on stage or starting a race.

b) **divert attention**. Focus your attention away from the provocation. Thus, if it is an individual, do not think of the person but rather concentrate on his tie. If you can find a gravy stain – so much the better!! Try and find something ridiculous or funny about the provocation.

c) **delay response**. Gain time. The old advice to count to ten is good. Or better still, count backwards from twenty. Try and put yourself into a position that slows down your actions, so picture yourself as a slow motion replay on television. It is also important to distance yourself from the situation, so you are not standing in front of the provocation, but are like a fly on the wall.

5. **Getting Rid of Anger** : This is separate from stages (2)-(4). In this stage you use your knowledge of your type(s) of anger **to get rid of the anger when you are not in the provocation situation.** This is like a practice, but it is different. In real life, you have to control your anger as (2)-(4), but in this stage you get rid of your anger so there is less anger for you to control. There are several techniques :

a) screaming as long as you can

b) take a cushion and write the provocation on it, then beat it against the floor, throw it around the room and finally jump up and down on it

c) find a special place where you can be yourself and express your helplessness and loss, for example, visit a pond and feed the ducks whilst you let yourself feel totally vulnerable.

6. **Avoiding Rumination** : Rumination is a lovely word. Cows feed then they lie down and chew the grass some twenty times or more. Many individuals do the same with their problems – they go over the same mouthful again and again and again... With the cow, there is an end after twenty times; with some humans, they can go over the same situation twenty times and make no progress. In fact, the problem becomes worse in that the individual now believes that there is no solution. **All of the effort has produced the result only that no progress can be made. This result simply produces more anger and the cycle is repeated.** Whenever you find yourself ruminating, you should use the techniques in (5). Rumination is sometimes described as "brooding". The analogy of a brooding hen which is irritable and wants to sit a long time on eggs to produce young chickens is quite apt. **You must not waste time and energy on rumination or brooding.**

SUMMARY

1. Anger is the second rung of the ladder. At this stage, it is possible to go back to being lifeless, or to progress to the next rung in the ladder.

2. Anger is a feeling of great annoyance with no particular objective and often serves no useful purpose. There are five main types of anger.

3. Repressed anger is when anger is a result of the individual not being able to control the situation. There is a need to regain the ability to control matters.

4. Misdirected anger is the classic situation of blaming the messenger because the message is disliked. There is a need to find the right target for the anger.

5. Avoiding anger is when the individual has repressed his/her true feelings. This anger may have serious long term effects on health.

6. Anger may accompany other negative emotions such as grief, fear, sadness and depression.

7. Anger may be appropriate to the circumstance, and is then the most useful.

8. There may be any combination of (3)–(7), and one combination may follow another.

9. The solution involves the knowledge of anger and its combinations, preparation for provocation, dealing with confrontation, using the **3D's blocking techniques**, getting rid of anger and avoiding rumination.

CHAPTER FIVE

DENIAL

William John Cavendish Bentwick Scott, the fifth Duke of Portland was born in 1800 AD. He lived a normal, aristocratic life until 1854 when he inherited the title and Welbeck Abbey in Nottinghamshire. The title, the property and the money allowed him to live out a bizarre lifestyle which denied the existence of the real world. Although this is a true story, many may believe that it is fantasy.

He wanted to deny the existence of daylight. He therefore built 15 miles of tunnels under his estate. Some of these tunnels were more than two carriages wide. Underground, he constructed the largest ballroom in the country, a billiard room that was large enough for a dozen billiard tables and a 250 feet square library. The underground ballroom had a lift which could take 20 people at a time, and two thousand people could have danced with ease under the giant chandeliers of the ballroom which had a ceiling painted to resemble a glowing sunset. All of this sounds like a marvellous adventure of an eccentric aristocrat. Unfortunately, the Duke was very shy and also rejected people. No one was invited to the ballroom and no one played on the billiard tables. He hated to have contact with people. He had a tunnel specially constructed between his house and the railway station so that he would not have to meet anyone.

He was said to be the finest judge of horses in England. In Welbeck, he held perhaps the best 100 horses in the land. He built a windowless horse school, the second largest in England. Yet he never rode a single horse, and no one ever went to the school. His involvement was theoretical, he did not feel it necessary to face reality. In his 80th year, the Duke died. His cousin inherited the title and property. He found that the Great Hall of the Abbey had no floors. All of the Abbey's great treasures (paintings, carpets, furniture, luxuries) were crammed together in a few rooms. The dead Duke had also rejected all of the beauty of worldly treasures. His life was most unusual : he had everything but used his wealth to reject what he had and create fantasy.

-o-0-o-

Observation

Denial is the refusal to believe what is apparent. During a crisis, it is a very common stage, but fortunately, it is usually temporary. The situation with the fifth Duke of Portland was extreme. He denied the existence of daylight and the world as we know it. Nevertheless, this story demonstrates what an individual is capable of doing if given unlimited resources. **For most of us, it is good fortune that we do not have such resources as we are brought back to reality sooner** and we are forced to live in the real world by events and those around us. Facing the truth has never been easy and it is far worse when the truth is painful. Yet, like the man who hates daylight, one either has to face it or have the ability to dig 15 miles of tunnels in which to hide.

CASE HISTORIES

CASE ONE

Life should have been good for Douglas. He was 67 years old, retired with a generous pension. Then he heard that his 27 year-old daughter, Jennifer, had suddenly gone missing. Apparently, she had had a violent row with her boyfriend, had dashed out of the house and now had been missing for two weeks. The police had been informed, but after taking statements from everyone, they only reassured Douglas that most missing persons eventually returned home. This was not good enough for Douglas. He was close to his daughter and was determined to find her. He could not accept the police's advice to wait at home until his daughter contacted him.

He went out into the streets to search for his beloved daughter. As he walked, the pain of his loss was heavy and he felt as though he was carrying a rucksack with 50 kilograms on his shoulders. Occasionally, he would see someone who looked like his daughter, but whenever he got close it was someone else. Reflections in store windows, a voice or a familiar set of clothes, they all somehow reminded him of his daughter. But on careful examination, it was not her. Eventually, his endless walking of the streets was beginning to take its toll. A chest infection started and within two days he was confined to bed, hardly able to move.

In bed, his will to live seemed to fade away. He was tired, ill and in pain. Yet he was angry at the police for not doing more to find his daughter. And from his bed, he would

53

telephone the police 4–5 times a day. He would also insist on speaking to a senior officer to vent his anger. Then one day as usual when he requested a senior officer, he heard the voice at the other end of the telephone shouting :

"Can you get the officer on duty? It's that old geezer with the lost daughter. Mind you, if I was his daughter, I would probably run away as well!"

Douglas was shocked, he put the telephone down and he never telephoned the police again. Instead, he concentrated on getting better. When he was well, he went back to his gardening. A year later he won a flower competition with his contribution – a beautifully fragrant rose called "Jennifer".

CASE TWO

Life had not been easy for Claire. Everything had happened very quickly. She was 18 years old when her first child died. The reason was never truly explained, except that the doctors thought it was a "cot death". Claire was devastated. Slowly, she became angry with the doctors for not telling her and warning her about cot death. She was also angry with her husband because he had done nothing to prevent the disaster. He was also trying to adjust to normal life without recognizing that life would never be the same again. She just could not understand how he could be so stupid.

A month later, she still could not believe that her daughter had died. She would waken in the middle of the night quite certain that she had heard her daughter cry out. Only the continuing silence and her daughter's empty cot would bring her back to reality. Even when the door bell rang she would expect that it would be the police to say that her daughter was really alive and that it had all been a terrible mistake. She could not see how unlikely this was to happen. Throughout all of this, her husband was outstanding : kind, attentive and happy to do all the housework. Then, one morning over breakfast, Claire was about to shout at her husband when she saw him. For the first time in months she saw her husband : his hair was dishevelled, he had cut himself shaving and his shirt was dirty. As she looked at him, he glanced up at her and smiled. As she gazed at him, a tear ran down her cheek and she slowly returned his smile.

COMMENT

These two cases demonstrate the feelings of being lifeless and the anger that can follow great loss. This anger is often followed by denial. Through denial the person wants to put things right, to have the original situation. Sadly, life has moved on. To progress to the next rung of the ladder, there is a need to overcome denial. This is not easy, especially as denial is reassuring and comforting. Unfortunately, life is hard. Late at night after you have had many alcoholic drinks, your problems can disappear, but what happens in the morning? **You will have to look at yourself in the mirror and deal with your problems without the support of make-believe.**

MAJOR FACTORS

Denial is a strong word and means "the rejection of a

truth", "to refuse to agree", or "a refusal to acknowledge a truth". Perhaps the best example of denial is in the Bible. Jesus was speaking to his disciples on the eve of his crucifixion and predicted that his disciples would deny him. Peter was quick to reply :

"Even if all fall away on account of you, I never will" (Matthew 26, v33).

Jesus replied :

"This very night before the cock crows, thou shalt deny me thrice".

Peter replied :

"Though I should die with thee, yet will I not deny thee".

Later that evening, Jesus was arrested and Peter followed Him to the court of the High Priest. There, Peter was accused of being one of Jesus' followers but he denied this by saying :

"I don't know what you're talking about".

Twice more Peter denied Jesus with a final comment of :

"I don't know the man!" (Matthew 26, v74)

Immediately a cock crowed and Peter remembered Jesus' prediction and repented bitterly.

Yet, Peter was the first named of all the disciples and was the "rock" on which the church was built.

This story shows the strength of denial and how we are unable to control our reactions. It perhaps is best that we are aware of how we may easily deny the truth when we feel threatened. The emotion of denial is so strong that even when denying the existence of a truth, one is unaware of lying. With denial, there is an inability to see and think properly. The individual is suffering from such a painful loss that nothing else can be appreciated.

There are several important components of denial :

1. **Facts** : The facts of a person's situation cannot be faced. Despite all of the available, often overwhelming evidence, the person keeps denying and saying "It's not true". There is evidence that a loved one has died or left. Yet the individual keeps expecting to see, hear or have the loved one return. Alternatively, there could be bank statements showing that someone is bankrupt, yet, the person keeps hoping and saying, "Where could all the money have gone? There must be some mistake". **The denial of a loss is so strong that no evidence is good enough, apparently conflicting evidence is simply "not true".**

2. **Feelings** : As perception of the facts is distorted, so the person's emotions are equally affected. There is a feeling of being distant from the situation like being a fly on the wall. One feels detached, not responsible for one's actions as if looking on from the outside. Feelings are not only subdued, but there is also the belief that something is wrong. The person would frequently say, "This is not happening to me. There must be some mistake". **There is denial of true feelings and the person instead loses the ability to appreciate what is happening to her/him.**

3. **Others** : As the facts and feelings are being denied, the person's relationships with others are seriously affected. There is suspicion and even paranoia; there is a conviction that everyone is talking about the person. Others cannot be trusted. Even good friends can be given only limited time so that the conversation can never become personal. New acquaintances and

friends are preferred because they do not ask questions and accept what they are told. The person starts to behave as though he/she were in a foreign country. **They appear to be lost, without landmarks and surrounded by new people whose behaviour is unpredictable.** Understandably, it is very easy to become totally isolated, yet, the individual would often welcome isolation as a solution to their problems.

4. **Reality** : Denial of facts, feelings and individuals around the person, is simply a denial of the real world. Reality is lost and the person may often say "I'm dreaming". Although it feels like a dream, if they pinch themselves they will not wake up. It is very difficult to live in the real world and yet deny its existence. To do this, individuals often behave as though they are in a bubble which protects them from the world. They hear and see the world, but in their own bubble they see and feel things differently. Every now and then, they may let someone into their bubble for a few minutes. These are rare moments as it can be a mistake to let others get too close. Predictably, it is in these moments that the person is most vulnerable and when the bubble may burst. **It is possible to live many years denying the existence of the real world, protected by a personal bubble.** How does one get away from such a desperate situation? Why is it so difficult to replace the unreal with reality? How can one get inside someone else's bubble?

THE SOLUTION

Denial is a difficult stage of the ladder. **You feel that**

58

there are no answers to problems but instead there are more questions. Thus, a loss is denied, all the evidence of the loss is rejected and the inevitable conclusion is the loss did not happen. To live and grow, you must accept the reality. **The key to moving on from the process of denial is to know why there was denial.** To move to the next rung of the ladder involves an understanding of the importance of :

1. **Knowledge** : There is the old saying :
   "It is not the things you don't know that get you into trouble; it's the things you are certain about that are not true".
   Denial comes into this category. You are absolutely convinced that you are right. Yet all of the available evidence is against you. Reality has been turned into your desires. But why do honest and sincere people suddenly start to deny the truth? The answer is simple. **Denial gains time and provides short-term relief.** With denial, there is no need to face reality and so you have some more time to adjust to a great loss. Sadly, this is only a brief reprieve. If you can recognize that one is denying to gain time and relief from loss, then denial is easier to come to terms with and recognize.

2. **Time** : In the modern world we want everything now. And we can have so much now : strawberries in winter, pineapples in temperate countries and a microwave that can produce meals in minutes. But there are some things that take time. It has been found that patients with infections that produce severe pneumonia can be treated by antibiotics against the infection. The infection disappears but the patients

can take as long to recover as if they were not treated. **The explanation is that the body takes its own time. In the past, people recognized that it took time to recover from loss or illness.** There was a period of "mourning" or "convalescence". People wore black and everyone respected their space and condition. Alternatively, they went to a hospital in the country to recover, and were given space and time to heal. Sadly, in the world today, we simply do not give ourselves enough time to adjust to great loss. Thus, when you are in the stage of denial, **you need to have the knowledge of why it is happening and also that it may take some time.**

3. **Acceptance** : To move on to the next rung of the ladder and to climb out of the pit of life, you need to accept the truth. This is very difficult. **It is a time when you emotionally need the loss, but it is a time to accept the loss.** The earlier you can start to face the truth the better. This is because it takes time to adjust to the truth. Denial is like rust on the car, you remove it and paint over it but several weeks later, it appears again. You try many times. Eventually, you get serious and do a really good job and remove all of the rust until there is only bare metal, when you paint over it the rust does not appear again. **Do not be afraid that it takes many attempts to deal with denial.** Denial is like a comfortable bed, whereas truth appears to be a bed of stone. As many have found over the centuries, a bed of stone is not necessarily a total disaster and indeed can be the best remedy for a bad back. However there are far better reasons to accept the truth. Acceptance of truth heralds a way of life, Keats said :

"Beauty is truth, truth is beauty – that is all
Ye know on earth, and all ye need to know."
Thus, the truth is about how you want to live your life. Similarly, you must consider if you do not want truth, what are the consequences? Falsehood is a heavy burden, Saadi has commented :

"The telling of a falsehood is like the cut of a sabre; for though the wound may heal, the scar of it will remain".

SUMMARY

1. Denial is the refusal to believe what is apparent.

2. Facts are rejected. Denial of a loss is so strong an emotion that no evidence is good enough, all evidence is regarded as simply "not true".

3. As facts are distorted, your feelings are equally affected. You lose the ability to appreciate what is happening to you.

4. Relationships with others are also affected. New friends are chosen as they do not ask questions. You become lost, without landmarks and surrounded by new people whose behaviour is unpredictable.

5. Reality is denied. You appear to be in a bubble protected from the real world. Everything is distorted.

6. The solution is to have knowledge that denial is an essential part of your ability to deal with loss and it must be recognized.

7. Denial gains time and provides short-term relief. It needs much time and may require several attempts to adjust to a great loss.

8. To move to the next rung of the ladder, you have the difficult but essential step of accepting the truth.

CHAPTER SIX

DISGRACE

"Gordon Bennett!!" The expression is usually said with great feeling and often refers to something outrageous and disgraceful. Considering the origins of the term, current usage probably does not do the term credit. James Gordon Bennett was a man who lived a quite incredible life. He was born on 10th May 1841, but by the time he was 27 years old he owned the New York Tribune newspaper and was very, very rich. Although he was a very flamboyant character, he had great vision and was a co-founder of the Associated Press News Agency which had world-wide news coverage. Yet, for a man with such great achievements, it is for his excesses and disgrace that he is principally remembered.

In 1876 he became engaged to the beautiful, rich Caroline May. The pair were the talk of the town and every man envied Gordon Bennett. But the relationship was doomed. On New Year's day in 1877, Caroline's father held a huge, lavish party. Everyone who was anyone attended. Preparations took months and the food took weeks to prepare. It was the special event of the decade. Gordon Bennett ruined it all. Just before midnight, he mistook the fireplace for a toilet. Caroline's family were disgraced and Gordon had to fight a duel with her brother. Further, he became a social outcast, and had to flee to Paris.

In Paris, his behaviour continued in an uncontrolled way.

He would attend the very best restaurants, such as Maxime's, with the most beautiful women. But at the end of the evening, he would be drunkenly tossing bottles across the room or picking fights with the other diners. Yet, he had class and would always pay double the cost of the damages. Even with money, his behaviour was outrageous. One night, he amazed everyone in the restaurant by burning thousands of francs because the wad of notes in his back pocket was too large and uncomfortable.

In 1877, he built a yacht, the Lysistrata at a cost of millions of francs. On board, he had every comfort. Not only did he have a full-scale Turkish bath, but he also had masseurs on call 24 hours a day. In addition, there was a special padded room holding an Alderney cow so that he could have fresh milk. Every day, a servant was detailed to make fresh butter and brandy milk punch. Nevertheless, Gordon Bennett was blessed with good health. At the age of 73 years, he married Baroness de Reuter of the Reuters News Agency. He died four years later having had a full and rich life in which he had spent several fortunes.

-o-0-o-

Observation

Gordon Bennett was a gifted and talented man. His life was full of great achievements and success. Yet, there was also much disgrace. His excesses were extraordinary, outrageous and very memorable. Disgrace can be most interesting to others and not readily forgotten. Fewer people are remembered for their successes compared to those who are identified with their disgrace. Whenever there is great loss, it can be perceived that there is great disgrace. However, great loss and disgrace occurs in only a few situations but especially in those individuals with a high profile. For most, the perception of disgrace is greatest in their own minds; to the rest of the world, there is often little interest as the situation is not sufficiently outrageous or memorable. **Thus for the vast majority, their personal loss is NOT a disgrace as perceived by others.** Indeed, for most situations, if the truth is told, the individual will receive sympathy and support.

CASE HISTORIES

CASE ONE

Michael was a successful accountant with his own business, and at 50 years of age, had also been a local councillor for 25 years. His integrity and honesty appeared beyond dispute; he was a man of principles and had a social conscience. Then one night, at a public meeting he was accused of fiddling his expenses over many years. Michael was flabbergasted, and stormed out of the meeting. Over the ensuing weeks the facts were slowly released to the press, and there was even mention of expensive visits to foreign nightclubs at the taxpayers' expense.

Predictably after his initial shock, Michael reacted angrily to the accusations and denied everything. He took out libel actions against newspapers and radio stations. It all became very messy. In spite of pleading his innocence,

65

he was forced to resign. His business went downhill and his wife left him. The shame and disgrace followed him everywhere. He took to staying at home behind drawn curtains with a large bottle of brandy. It looked as though it could not get worse, but then one night he fell asleep in the lounge and his smouldering cigar started a fire. The house burned down and he was admitted to hospital with severe burns.

As he lay in the hospital bed, he felt old and tired. For weeks, he had no visitors. Then one day, Brian, his political opponent in the council came to see him. Michael was beaten:

"Brian, have you come here to gloat?"

Brian slowly bowed his head and replied :

"No. No, Michael I have not come here to gloat. Over the years, you have always beaten me in every argument. I have always admired and envied you".

Brian then slowly placed a large bunch of flowers on the table and left.

Michael reached for the card on the flowers. The card had a simple message :

"For a man who can make things happen".

The next day Michael called a press conference. He admitted his mistakes and promised to put things right. He rebuilt his life and repaid all his debts. It took him 10 years.

CASE TWO

Julie was Head Girl at the local school. She was pretty, popular, good at sports and clever, with a bright future. She was given an excellent offer from a good university.

Everything was going to plan. Her life appeared to have gold dust sprinkled on it. Then came the exams and months later, the results. She had failed everything. No one could believe it. Julie simply locked herself in her room and cried. Then, she appealed against the results, but the results were confirmed. Two months later, her friends went to universities throughout the land, and Julie went back to school. People looked at her, but instead of smiling they were embarrassed. She used her anger to work and to work; and she spent her lunch break walking far away from the school, eating an apple. She lost her ability to smile; and her loneliness and isolation were obvious to everyone. It appeared that she was denying that this could happen to her. Yet, the facts were clear : she had failed. Her dreams were destroyed, her disgrace public and complete.

Then, one day whilst she was out walking, a second year student came up to her and offered her an apple. Julie was taken aback : this was the first day for weeks that she was not eating an apple during the lunch break. She smiled, hesitantly at first, but later a very broad and enthusiastic smile. She thanked the girl before taking a big bite. She then asked :

"How did you know I had forgotten my apple today?"

The girl quickly replied :

"That's easy. I follow you every day and eat my apple when you eat yours".

Julie was astounded and asked :

"But why?"

"Oh, I have to, was the reply, "When I came to this school last year, I was afraid and you helped me. Now, you are afraid and I have to help you".

Julie could not remember helping the girl, but then a

year ago she was a celebrity. Now, she was almost alone. They shared the apple and remained friends for life.

COMMENT

Disgrace and shame are very strong emotions, most often, experienced by individuals with a high profile, though anyone may be involved. **Whereas overcoming denial is personal, disgrace is the public's perception of your loss.** This is quite different to coming to terms with your own shortcomings. As it is public, you are not in control and are vulnerable. You have to trust the goodwill of others. It is noteworthy that in both of these cases, great support and regard were demonstrated by those around : In Case One, it was an opponent; and in Case Two, it was someone who had remembered a kindness. Whilst one is in disgrace, **it is both the good and the bad of our past that catches up with us.** How do you progress to the next rung of the ladder? How do you overcome the humiliation, shame and disgrace? Can you avoid disgrace?

MAJOR FACTORS

Someone with grace shows a "pleasing quality". As with grace, when one is in disgrace, one's actions and behaviour are still observed. There is much pressure on the individual and those around are observing one's response. It is reminiscent of J. Lawton's poem, "When the pressure's on" :

68

"How do you act
When the pressure's on,
When the chance
For Victory's almost gone?
When Fortune's star
Has refused to shine,
When the ball
Is on your five-yard line?

How do you act
When the going's rough?
Does your spirit lag
When breaks are tough?
Or is there in you
A flame that glows
Brighter as fiercer
The battle grows?

How hard, how long
Will you fight the foe?
That's what the world
Would like to know!
Cowards can fight
When they're out ahead;
The uphill grind
Shows a thoroughbred!

You wish for a success?-
Then tell me, Son,
How do you act
When the pressure's on?

Disgrace is commonly believed to be "a condition of
shame", "loss of reputation" or "dishonour", (New Collins
Concise English Dictionary, 1988). However, more

literally, disgrace is defined in the Shorter Oxford English Dictionary (1983) as "to undo or mar the grace of" or "to disfigure". **The essence of all of these definitions is that it is how one is perceived by the rest of the community.** It is therefore a very similar process to denial (Chapter Five). With denial one faces the truth for oneself; with disgrace those around us face the truth. As these two processes are so similar, it will be approached in the same way. **The important factors in disgrace are :**

1. **Facts** : There can be great difficulties in persuading others of the truth. Others may refuse to believe what is being said, and reply "You are not that sort of person" or "I've known you all of my life, and you could not do that". There is a great temptation, in the face of such loyalty for the individual not to face the truth but to continue to voice their innocence. **Such a temptation must be resisted because the long term consequences will be far worse.** One needs to openly speak the truth as this process allows others to believe, and also helps one to face the facts of the situation. It also helps if the explanation is consistent rather than if it changes for each person. The same explanation reinforces its truth.

2. **Feelings** : Others will have as much difficulty coming to terms with the disgrace as the person involved. Very strong feelings are part of the explanation, however, there is also the fact that the person's disgrace will show that those around had shown poor judgement. They will feel betrayed. Many might become nasty and be vindictive. **There can be a great desire to make the person suffer publicly for**

the disgrace. Such strong emotional feelings can be very frightening and destructive; nothing can be worse than a friend who then becomes an enemy.

3. **Others** : There is the saying that "other people either think of you as better than you are or worse than you are, but only you yourself know what you are". Disgrace is about what others think of the truth. Some will be understanding and sympathetic, whilst others will be hurtful and destructive. For a while the person is under the magnifying glass and all of his/her actions are carefully examined. It is a great test of a person's character and resolve. At this time, as the person is subjected to the opinions of all of those around, it may be useful to remember the comment by J. G. Holland: "No one can disgrace us but ourselves".

4. **Reality** : Whilst the community comes to a conclusion on a person's loss, the person's position in the community is suspended. It is not unlike being suspended from work on full pay whilst the situation is being investigated. It also has similar disadvantages : one is under suspicion and told to stay away. In the Chapter on Denial (Chapter Five), individuals place themselves in a bubble separated from the community. The reverse happens in disgrace, now the **community places the individual in a glass bubble and everyone looks on eagerly.** As with denial, the community often delays facing reality.

THE SOLUTION

Disgrace can be like being lifeless (Chapter Three). You

are totally numbed and in shock. Indeed, some individuals can progress up the ladder quite positively, but when they reach the stage of "disgrace", it all becomes too much and they regress back to being lifeless. Such a reaction is sad, as **if you can overcome disgrace, you are nearly out of the pit of life.** In many ways, disgrace is the darkest hour and the most difficult stage of the ladder. The reason is that with disgrace, you can do nothing but accept other people's reactions. To deal with disgrace you need to be passive and you cannot do much to influence matters. **It is by being totally vulnerable and trusting in those around you that you progress to the next rung of the ladder.** The need to be so open is the main obstacle in reaching the next stage. You might feel that it is asking too much to turn your other cheek and allow someone to hurt you again. **Yet, when you can display such trust, it is a mark of your strength (and not weakness).** To move to the next rung of the ladder involves :

1. **Knowledge :** The most important bit of knowledge is **to recognize that disgrace is not the end but is only a part of the process of getting out of the pit.** As you are living in a community, it is important for there to be a stage when the community considers your loss. For a very few, this is unthinkable and they may be forced into lifelessness, isolation or suicide. However, for most, there are enough in the community who offer support and sympathy for you to cope with the situation. The generosity of spirit of others, especially those who appear to be enemies, must never be underestimated. Life is always a mixture of emotions, and with disgrace there is always some grace present. It is not unlike the saying :

"Some people complain because roses have thorns; rather be thankful that thorns have roses". In coping with disgrace, you may be injured by the thorns, but try and enjoy the beauty and fragrance of the rose.

2. **Time** : When there has been a significant change of position, there needs to be time to adjust. It is so if someone is promoted to a better job, wins a fortune or otherwise experiences good fortune. This is the positive side, but the same applies to the negative side of life. So, as with bad luck, **with disgrace there also needs to be a period of adjustment.** You need to have some space to consider the situation again. Usually, there are only minor adjustments to be made before life can carry on as before. However, sometimes the loss can be substantial and the disgrace overwhelming. In these cases, there needs to be a recognition that **no matter how bad the situation, it will improve with time.** This is because these situations appear worse than they are. In addition, we often make the mistake of thinking that a person can deal with sudden good fortune, such as winning £18 million on the national lottery. Yet we underestimate a person's capacity to deal with a great loss. In reality, both scenarios are equally difficult to deal with, and require considerable time and energy. Remember when adjusting to a great loss that "Patience is the best medicine".

3. **Acceptance** : If you can accept disgrace, it is possible to move to the next stage. Some individuals feel that they should accept disgrace as a "punishment". I feel that this is wrong. **Disgrace is simply a result of**

how your actions are perceived. In some circumstances, if the full facts were known, the conclusion might be different. We are all a mixture of good and bad; honourable and dishonourable. These are two sides of the coin. Many would like to look at just one side of the coin. So be it. However, to understand the good a person does, one may need to see the person's bad side; to understand honourable behaviour one may need to recognize that the person may also act dishonourably. Yet, perhaps for those in disgrace, one should remember Plautus :

"Whatever disgrace we may have deserved, it is almost always in our power to re-establish our character".

SUMMARY

1. To overcome the stage of denial is personal, however, disgrace is the community's perception of your loss.

2. Others may have great difficulty in facing the truth of your disgrace as it can show them having made poor judgement. Alternatively, there can be a great desire by others to make you suffer.

3. For a while, your actions will be carefully examined. The community places you in a glass bubble and looks at your behaviour.

4. If you can overcome disgrace, you are nearly out of the pit of life. To deal with disgrace, you need to be totally vulnerable and trusting in those around you.

5. The solution of how you should deal with disgrace depends on recognizing the importance of knowledge, time and acceptance.

6. You should have the knowledge that disgrace is not the end, but is only part of the process of getting out of the pit.

7. You need time for you and others to adjust to the changed circumstances, and to strong feelings about your loss.

8. You must accept disgrace and remember that it is almost always within our power to re-establish our good reputation.

CHAPTER SEVEN

ENDEAVOUR

Barnes Neville Wallis was born in 1887 and will always be remembered as the man who invented the "bouncing bomb". However, his life was far more than just one invention. He was a man who lived his life with "endeavour", he tried and he tried again all through his long life.

At the age of 79 years, he was interviewed for a BBC documentary. The interviewer was astonished that Wallis was then involved in a project for an aircraft which could fly at great heights (over 250,000 feet) and at great speed (about 12,000 miles per hour). It was a design for an aircraft that could leave Britain and reach Australia in one and a half hours. The interviewer could not believe it and said :

"Is this not a tremendous step forward? We have Concorde as our fastest plane and it can only travel at 1,500 miles per hour. You say that your plane can do 12,000 miles per hour. Is this not a bit too much ?"

"Yes, it is", Wallis replied, "But why not? Why not?"

He then proceeded to explain how it could be done. The interview was such a moving event that it was turned into a second documentary about Barnes Wallis and called : **"Why not? Why not?"** It was a tribute to a man who did not accept the obstacles that life put before him.

Wallis was a man of great humanity. The bouncing bomb

was designed to destroy two massive dams supplying water and hydroelectricity to German war factories in the Ruhr. Nineteen Lancasters, crewed by men of 617 Squadron, took off in the middle of the night on the mission. Sadly, eight Lancasters containing 56 men failed to return. Wallis was inconsolable and had to be sedated and put to bed. The events of that fateful night lived with him forever. After the war he started to design a swing-wing aircraft which could land with its wings extended, but fly faster than sound with wings tucked back. Prototypes performed well but Wallis would not risk a pilot's life to test the aircraft. The swing-wing project was eventually shelved. Wallis was furious and stormed into the civil servant's office and demanded an explanation. It is said that he was told :

"Only one in every hundred research projects stands a chance of succeeding, so I put all one hundred projects in the waste basket. This way I'm right 99% of the time".

Barnes Wallis persevered and 22 years later, the RAF took delivery of a swing-wing plane, the Tornado.

Wallis lived for 92 years and designed the R100 airship, the Wellington bomber, bouncing bombs and swing-wing aircraft. Once, he was asked if he despaired of all the obstacles that were put in his path, his response was characteristic :

"My dear fellow, the whole joy of life, as you must know in your own experience, is battle, not winning. Fighting for an idea is the joy of life".

-o-0-o-

Observation

Barnes Wallis was a real hero. He was a man who

understood that this life was about showing great endeavour – that life is about fighting and doing battle. **This was a man who was not easily discouraged, indeed, the more the obstacles the greater was his endeavour.** To progress up the ladder from the pit of life, one needs to show great endeavour. If such effort is demonstrated, the next rung of the ladder will be easily reached. **This chapter is about the stage in which one is required to work, to try, to endeavour.** The end is near, but much is now required.

CASE HISTORIES

CASE ONE

Sophie was a vivacious 60 year old business woman. She was both hard-working and very intelligent; she triumphed in a man's world, often because men under-estimated her. Her bright eyes and ready smile disguised a computer-like brain. All around her were in awe of her achievements. Life put her through the fire and she always managed to triumph. Then, she developed Post Viral Fatigue Syndrome (myalgic encephalomyelitis). She was broken; a woman like her could not afford to be ill.

She did not stay lifeless long and quickly became angry -angry that she should have to deal with this particular problem at this time of her life. At the same time, she denied the illness and tried to carry on. She excused her ill-health as "something that occasionally happens to me" – whatever that meant. Those around her tried to help, but she just slapped them down – she could destroy a strong man with a stare or a cutting sentence. People started to avoid her. This made matters worse because Sophie was a sociable, gregarious person and enjoyed the company of others. She was like a leaf being blown around the garden in autumn winds. Sophie's intelligence saved her. One day she sat back and looked at her situation, and realised that she had to stay within her energy limits. When Sophie made up her mind, things happened. Nothing would get in her way. She cancelled all of her social engagements, and dealt with the "disgrace" with great aplomb. This was a lady at work. Then, she focused her intelligence and energies on the problem in hand. She learnt the new rules of coping with her illness. It required great dedication and endeavour. She did all that was expected and more. Days were spent not in activity but sitting in the back garden, in full ski attire, watching the birds.

It was enough. She recovered by demonstrating that she could change and adapt to new rules. The entertaining of friends started again and she also was able to do much more, but something had changed. Experience of this illness was a turning point. For the rest of her life, Sophie continued her good deeds, but all commented on one major change. She, by watching the birds, had found a new kind of peace.

CASE TWO

At 25 years of age Alexander had a great life. Single, charming, athletic and with a well-paid job he had the world at his feet. Women were particularly attracted to his rugged good looks, and there seemed to be an endless stream of beautiful admirers. Alexander remained cool and somehow appeared to be on top of every situation. Then all suddenly changed. He was returning home late one evening when he was hit on the head from behind. He fell to the ground under a hail of kicks to his head and body. As he looked up, one of his muggers was staring him in the face with eyes full of hatred. Slowly he placed a knife on Alexander's cheek and made a zig-zag scar from his right ear lobe to his mouth. Alexander was transfixed and could not move; his black belt in judo was not worth the sweat. Fortunately, another kick to the head brought a welcome unconsciousness.

When he awoke in hospital, he was told he had had a fractured jaw, broken nose and scars requiring 100 stitches. He was shocked, frightened and scared. He remained in this state long after he was discharged from hospital and the scars had healed. All he could do was lock himself in his apartment and stare at the television screen. Visitors found that he would occasionally become angry at the lack of law and order in the country but more usually he said nothing. Every morning he would go to the mirror in the bathroom and look at his face, as though expecting that the scars would have disappeared overnight. The scars remained and were obvious even through his beard.

Then one day, whilst he was out shopping, he saw two men trying to snatch an old lady's handbag. His pent-up emotions were suddenly released and he ran after the muggers. Suddenly, he remembered his judo and attacked the men, injuring them. His actions were quickly picked up by the media. However, when he appeared on television, he showed the public his scars to demonstrate that both young and old were vulnerable, and he said that everyone had a responsibility to keep crime off the streets. His honesty and openness touched viewers, and he was bombarded by letters of support. He started a group of young people who wanted to remove crime from the streets. Within months, his life changed as he regained his vigour and started to work for his ideas. His scars were no longer signs of disgrace, but became symbols of the wrong of crime and violence.

COMMENT

In both of these cases, high achieving individuals found themselves in the pit of life. **Their previous accomplishments and abilities could not protect them from the full horror of the pit**. For both, it was necessary to slowly climb the ladder out of the pit. It was not easy; it was not nice. If there was another way, they would have found it, but the ladder is the only way out of the pit. However, **the ladder is individual and everyone approaches each stage in their own particular way.** Yet, for both they were able to make progress to the next rung of the ladder. How was this achieved? What characteristics does one need to progress from disgrace (Chapter Six)? How would you react? Would you be able to show great endeavour, and even use your disgrace as an advantage?

MAJOR FACTORS

Endeavour means "to try" or "to do", usually with an "aim" and as a result of "effort" and "labour". **Therefore**

81

endeavour is an active process in which the individual has to be making a substantial effort and to be striving for an objective. It is quite unlike the stage of disgrace (Chapter Six) in which one is coming to terms with others' behaviour. With the stage of endeavour you are in the driving seat and your actions are being carefully observed. **Your commitment, your effort and your labour will be assessed by the results**. It is worth remembering the poem by Robert Hamilton called "Sorrow":

> "I walked a mile with pleasure
> She chattered all the way
> But left me none the wiser
> For all she had to say.
>
> I walked a mile with sorrow
> And ne'er a word said she
> But oh the things I learned from her
> When sorrow walked with me."

The problem is at this stage of the ladder, the individual is usually tired. He or she has come a long way up the ladder, and there is the temptation to ask "why bother?" or say "I can't do any more, I've no energy". **Matters are further complicated because there are other significant factors :**

1. **Time** : Many people on the ladder out of the pit of life feel that they can take their own time, without remembering that time waits for no one. One is tired and struggling to get through each day, and forgetting that the days have turned into weeks and months. The inability to appreciate that much around one is

changing is a characteristic of someone dealing with a great loss. Whereas one is in a world of slow-motion: the rest of the society are in fast-forward. The results of these different approaches to time can be far-reaching : **others may perceive your lack of progress as being a reflection that you do not care, and they then cease to give you understanding and sympathy.** Sadly, you then perceive this situation as confirmation that you are alone and without friends. This puts you in another vicious circle as you do not have support, you move slower and take even more time.

2. **Self** : At this stage, the individual may also have considerable physical and emotional handicaps. For those recovering from disease or accidents, the body may not be able to function properly. **However, it is important to recognize that physical limitations need not prevent endeavour.** Indeed, endeavour can be seen as the triumph of life over apparent physical disabilities. Some of the most moving moments of life are when both man and animals triumph over physical handicaps. It is perhaps one of the reasons so many watch the end of the London marathon. Elbert Hubbard had a very nice way of putting things :

"God will not look you over for medals, degrees or diplomas, but for scars."

One should not be afraid of endeavour because of one's scars; indeed, scars can be a reflection of one's endeavour.

3. **Principles** : It is said :

"The character of a man is his principles drawn out

and woven into himself". **We are what we believe and what we endeavour for.** At a time of crisis, what we are is sorely tested. Unfortunately, at such a time, our judgement is often impaired. **There are two easy mistakes to make : adoption of false or adoption of convenient principles.** Adopting false principles is not usually intentional, it can simply reflect our inability to think properly. Yet suddenly, something which we would never have done previously is not only acceptable, but seems to be the only and right decision. Similarly, convenient principles may be adopted. One is so very tired, that it seems right to hurt someone else; the action is excused by, "they were going to get hurt anyway" or "it could have been a lot worse". **These actions are wrong and unacceptable. We live and die by our principles.**

Therefore, only principles that are true to our character must live on. We must have the strength to reject the false or convenient solution. At a time of weakness, it is truly noble when one can amass the courage to do what is right and good.

THE SOLUTION

Endeavour is a difficult rung of the ladder because it requires considerable commitment and action from you. It is also needed at a time when you are nearly out of the pit of life and you are tired and there seem to be strong reasons for giving up. The summit of the mountain is just above, but your body aches and complains; it would be easier to turn around and let gravity take you to the bottom of the mountain. Perhaps, you should recall

Ovid's observation :

"Either do not attempt at all, or go through with it".

At this rung of the ladder, the solution involves recognition of two significant factors : personal and social.

1. **Personal** : At a time when you are weak and looking for an easy option, there needs to be strong, principled action. It is easy to understand why so many fail at this stage, or take an excessive amount of time to move to the next rung of the ladder. There are three problems : you are tired; you are emotionally drained; and you cannot see reality. **Emotional exhaustion must not be underestimated as it makes people do what they would not otherwise do.** It is the principal weapon in some torture techniques, such as sleep deprivation. It is also used by religious fanatics to control their followers. **You need to make time to think, to analyze what you are doing and to test if this is true to your character.** At this stage, many hide themselves in activities so that they do not have to think. This is wrong and must be realised. **Ideally, you need to take 1–2 hours per day to think about your situation.** Unless you do this, you will be tempted by the easy option. Nothing in this world is easy and getting out of the pit is far from easy. You need now, more than ever, to act in ways that are true to yourself.

2. **Social** : We live in communities, and it is to be hoped once you are out of the pit of life, you will want to rejoin your community. People judge you by your actions, and only very rarely make allowances for your personal circumstances. **Other people have their**

own problems, and can give you only a small part of their time. Thus, you may be going through a major life crisis, but you are surrounded by people who cannot stop to watch a beautiful rainbow. If people are so busy that they cannot appreciate beauty, will they be concerned about your problems? No one has enough time for you, and they will still judge you harshly. The reason is just that you have failed and you have let the side down; in one or two years, they may do the same as you but that does not stop them hurting you now. You must simply get on with living your life according to your principles and let your actions speak for your character. It is said :

> "If through all his days, a man tells the truth as he sees it, keeps his word as he gives it, and works well at his task, he gets what is called a good reputation."

A good reputation is the end result of true endeavour, and there are no easy solutions.

SUMMARY

1. At this rung of the ladder, you are required to work, to try and to endeavour.

2. The ladder is individual and everyone approaches each stage in their own particular way, but previous accomplishments do not protect you from the misery of the pit.

3. Endeavour is an active process in which the individual

has to make a substantial effort, and to be striving for an objective.

4. Great commitment, effort and labour is required and you will be assessed by your results.

5. Problems in this stage include your perception of time, your physical and emotional limitations and your principles.

6. The solution involves your behaviour in two important areas : personal and social.

7. Personal behaviour must show that despite your emotional state, you make time to think, analyze what you are doing and to test if this is true to your character.

8. Social behaviour must include a recognition that other people have their own problems, and can give you only a small part of their time. Yet, your actions will be judged and people will take sides.

CHAPTER EIGHT

RENEWAL

Charles was a company director with a reputation for doing business aggressively. He was good at arguments and could turn any situation to his advantage. In addition, he was half Italian and was therefore emotional and demonstrative. Although he was a small man, when he shouted and glared, strong men were frightened. His family were also exasperated by his short fuse and his hatred of standing in queues or slow service. Since he could remember life, his son was always aware that his dad would walk out of a restaurant because of slow service. He also vividly recalled saying to his dad one evening, when they were out to celebrate his mother's birthday and the service was slow :

"Dad, it's Mom's birthday. We don't mind waiting. It's not nice to leave the restaurant now."

It was all to no avail and two minutes later the whole family were walking to a new restaurant.

Then one cold December day, Charles had a heart attack. This man who had believed himself to be immortal was shown to be human, and fragile. Suddenly, he was in great pain and could not care about his work. He was resigned to all of the investigations in hospital, and all of the results pointed to the same thing : Charles had to change his behaviour and become a different person. All of the doctors said this to him, and the family knew it to be true but all doubted his ability to change. Yet, Charles was an exceptional man, he could change if he wanted to. On discharge from hospital, he announced he would change. His family were pleased but still had their doubts. Two months went by and Charles did not have any arguments, but all felt that it was only a matter of time before he exploded.

It was on holiday in Germany when the family's opinion of Charles changed. The family had bought their bus tickets from the driver and had sat down. The driver had come back into the bus and shouted at Charles for not stamping his tickets in the bus. In the past, Charles would have exploded at the silly system which required you to buy your bus ticket from the driver, and then to have them stamped in the bus. Instead, Charles took his tickets to the machine and had them stamped. The bus driver was having a bad day, and continued to shout and complain about Charles' behaviour. The entire family was silent as they waited for Charles to explode. It did not happen. The incident was too much for the son, and when they got off the bus, he asked :

"Dad, why did you say nothing?"

His father stopped walking and said :

"Well, son, since my heart attack, I am a new man. I look at things differently now."

His son was impressed but persevered :

"Yes. I can see that, but how did you stop yourself losing your temper?"

His father took some time to answer, but then said :

"At first, it was difficult. But I then thought to myself if a man like that could live with himself for life, surely I can put up with him for a few minutes?"

-o-0-o-

Observation

The stage of renewal involves changing attitudes and lifestyles. **There has been a great loss and to cope means that there needs to be great changes.** For many around the affected individual, there will be the belief that change is not possible. But as Longfellow said :

> "All things must change, to something new, to something strange."

We must not underestimate someone's ability to change. **It is simply a matter of how much that individual wants to be different.** If there is commitment, then everything is possible. It may be new and strange, but it can happen. The age of the person does not matter. Old or young, the important consideration is simply a desire to be different because of the loss suffered.

CASE HISTORIES

CASE ONE

Marion was someone special. She had spent the best years of her life looking after her mother. Although she had brothers and sisters, it was left to her to care for her invalid mother. She had resigned herself to her situation and was happy to sacrifice her own happiness. Then suddenly her mother died, and at 42 years old, Marion found herself alone. Too old to have children and too young for a pension; she was desolate when she thought of the long lonely years ahead of her. She was numbed, lifeless. After the funeral, Marion became angry: with her brothers and sisters for their selfishness; at her mother for being an invalid; and with herself for all of the wasted years of her life. Yet, her routine, looking after her mother, was ingrained in her consciousness. She found herself boiling two eggs in the morning or making two mugs of chocolate in the evening. In desperation, she decided to visit her brothers and sisters.

The visits were most revealing : she realised that her siblings pitied her and could not appreciate her sacrifice; they felt that it was her duty as they had so much more important things in their lives. Marion returned home greatly saddened, but slowly she realised that she had cared for her mother for herself and not for her brothers and sisters. Love is about giving and sacrifice, and not about taking and self-indulgence. She then felt proud, proud of the way she was living and proud of what she had done. She started a business course at the local college. Then she opened a business selling knitwear and her special jams and preserves. All of the years that she had cared for her mother were not wasted. She had learned to knit wonderful clothes and her cooking was superb. Her business flourished. Five years later, a rich American walked into her shop. They chatted and he tasted her jam. They had dinner and he looked into her eyes. He saw strength, suffering and sacrifice, and he could not resist his feelings. He felt that he was looking into a deep, blue lagoon without a bottom which pulled him into itself. He was totally captivated. They were married within a month.

CASE TWO

Harry was a 15 year old schoolboy. He was not exceptional, but was totally happy being just ordinary. He did not mind others around him who were successful, indeed he admired them. Harry was just happy being Harry. Then after a short illness, he was diagnosed as having leukaemia. Everyone was shocked. This could not happen to gentle Harry who did no wrong to anyone. If there was a God, how could he do it to Harry? Or perhaps, the doctors had made a mistake and Harry was really okay. Sadly, there was no mistake and Harry had a severe form of leukaemia. He had six months to live or if he was lucky, a year. Treatment started and Harry lost his hair. It was bad timing, there was a round of Christmas parties and so Harry had to turn up with a "bonnet" to hide his baldness. He felt odd and out of place. His friends saw a different Harry, one with courage and strength – someone who anyone could admire. His friends knew that they could not come to terms with Harry's situation. Most important, they started to recognize how precious life was; life was a precious gift which must not be taken for granted. Somehow Harry recognized the predicament of his friends, and had a series of jokes about bald-headed men. His favourite was : "Most people have to wait until they are 40 years to be bald. As I am special, it happens at 15 years!!"

Whilst Harry was at the hospital having treatment, he met Louise. She was a 9 year old with childhood leukaemia. As they talked, Harry was amazed at her maturity and compassion. Often she would spend most of the time discussing his problems. When Harry asked about her life, she would reply : "I don't have too many problems. I am not old enough to have a complicated life, but I would like a doll's house in the garden." Harry was humbled. He was worrying about all of his missed opportunities and here was someone in a similar position who wanted a doll's house. Harry decided to build Louise the best doll's house possible. He started collecting money and even got his friends to work for this project. Harry wrote letters to everyone he could think of and spent the rest of the time designing the house himself. The money was quickly raised, but then Harry spent the time supervising the builders. After a month, a superb doll's house which could accommodate Louise's wheel-chair was built. There was a civic opening of the house as it had caught the imagination of the whole community. But it was not the cameras or the press that made the event memorable, it was the simplicity of Louise's smile.

COMMENT

Both Marion and Harry realised that despite the circum-stances, they needed to go through a process of renewal. **Through renewal, there is consolidation of the progress already made in climbing out of the pit of life.** Renewal involves a commitment to life – to reaffirm one's beliefs so that one does not slip back down the ladder. It is a high point when one makes state-ments that reflect one's innermost feelings. **It is quite simply the way that one wants to live.** This is a difficult stage of the ladder because it involves action. It is about how one acts in the face of one's loss. **It can be noble or it can be vindictive.** So, how do some people act in a way that inspires those around them? And how do some individuals act in a way that destroys everything? More importantly, how would you act? And what would be your most important considerations?

MAJOR FACTORS

Each year, spring renews the land from the winter's cold. During winter, one can become depressed and fear that spring will never come. The cycle of the seasons should remind us that great loss also will eventually be replaced. William Cowper had a nice way of saying this:

> "If winter bellow from the north,
> Soon the sweet spring comes dancing forth,
> And nature laughs again.
> What if thine heaven be overcast?
> The dark appearance will not last,
> Expect a brighter sky."

Renewal means "to begin again" or to "make a new start". The process of endeavour (Chapter Seven) involves activity and can be very difficult for many individuals. However, **the process of renewal is even more difficult as it involves a change of mental attitude to consolidate the previous successes in climbing the ladder.** This change of outlook will also affect how the individual sees life and their place in it. **Renewal therefore involves a different way of living as a result of a changed mental attitude.** This new approach can result in not only real healing but new growth which can prevent slipping backwards. It is part of development and will ensure that the individual comes out of the pit of life. **There are several important factors :**

1. **Dependence** : We live in a world where others and machines solve our problems. If the sink is blocked,

one gets the plumber to fix it; if one is cold, the switch of the central heating can solve the problem. **It is easy to be dependent on others to deal with life's difficulties.** On many occasions, one can actually feel that you own someone else – a wife must stay in the marriage, a son must not leave home, an employer cannot get rid of an employee. These attitudes may also be a result of the community one lives in where the State looks after the individual. **Whenever there is loss, dependence increases as one is more vulnerable and less capable of looking after oneself.** This dependence can be a great obstacle to progress out of the pit. Simply, one is waiting on others for help. One is sitting at the side of the road waiting for a lift. Great journeys are made by walking and not waiting.

2. **Replacements** : In the chapter on denial (Chapter Five), the individual comes to terms with the truth and does not cling to the hope that there has not been a loss. Often **the individual may try to find a quick replacement.** Thus, if a pet dies in an accident, the owner quickly goes out and buys a replacement. Whereas this is possible for a pet, it is not as simple to replace a spouse or child. Even if it is possible to find a replacement, it is usually not the best solution. To get out of the pit, requires significant changes in the person and a replacement can interfere with real progress. Young children know this. Many parents have tried to replace an old battered teddy bear with a large new one, but the child has rejected the new toy. **When we lose our possessions they cannot easily be replaced even though the replacement is newer and apparently better.**

3. **The Past :** To get to this stage of the ladder has required considerable perseverance. However, even among the best, there is a tendency to slip into the past – to think of how things used to be and dream of the good times. **Renewal is the last rung of the ladder, and it is here that there is the final look back at the past.** One is on a ship that is heading out to sea; but first before the land of previous good times disappears, one needs to look back, wave and shed a tear. Unlike denial (Chapter Five), one is not going to dwell in the past; instead one is moving forwards and the past is disappearing into the sunset. Many are afraid of their constant reminders of the past, but there is nothing to fear. The past is real and cannot be ignored; the only mistake is if one felt trapped in the past. Thus, the past has to become an integral part of our living in the present.

THE SOLUTION

The last rung of the ladder can be the most difficult. It is like the night being darkest just before the dawn -**when you feel that exhausted by all your efforts and it is time to give up.** Similarly, with the last rung of the ladder, a final effort is required. Even though you are tired, **it is time to adopt the following :**

1. **Responsibility :** In life, perhaps the most difficult thing to recognize is that we are all individually responsible for ourselves. Although **it is convenient to depend on others, ultimately you need to take responsibility for yourself.** Shaw explains the position beautifully :

96

"Liberty means responsibility. That is why most men dread it."

To be free is to climb out of the pit of life; freedom is to take responsibility for yourself. For many this can be particularly difficult, especially if you have depended on others all of your life. **You have to recognize that the prize is great : your independence and liberty.** No great prize is attained without a struggle and a fight.

2. **Living Without :** You need not to want to find quick replacements for your loss. As with many hurried substitutes, the product is usually grossly inferior. **It is often better to have nothing at all than a poor substitute.** To understand this you need to have the strength to live without something. It can seem daunting and even impossible, however, it is often very easy and satisfying. We tend to feel that nothing should change in our lives. Yet, when change comes it can teach us, make us happier and stronger. Sadly, it takes a large amount of trust at this stage to let life take its natural course, you should remember that it is easier to go with the flow of life than to fight against life. **When you learn to live without, you start to become strong.**

3. **Finding Yourself :** Life is full of so much which is lost – opportunities, friends, possessions and the past. Yet, you are fortunate if you have a lot to lose. Nevertheless, sometimes you find something which was important but got lost. **For many who are going through a crisis, the most important thing to find is yourself.** This seems almost a stupid statement, but it is at times of crisis that most people panic and

behave in an unnatural way. The few who are strong retain their identity. The lucky can find themselves again, and it is a great discovery. Life is so fast that often you are conditioned to live in a particular way, and you are too busy to ask yourself if this is what you want. **Renewal is when you rediscover yourself, and you may not be what you used to be but what you have become as a result of your loss.** It is a precious journey and must not be resisted, especially as the results are usually gratifying.

SUMMARY

1. As you have had a great loss, there needs to be great changes if you are to cope. Do not underestimate your ability to change; it is only a matter of how much you want to change.

2. With renewal, there is consolidation of the progress already made in climbing out of the pit of life. Renewal can be noble or it can be vindictive.

3. The process of renewal involves a different way of living as a result of a changed mental attitude.

4. The problems at this stage are that there is : a great dependence on others; a temptation to try and find a replacement for the loss; and a feeling of a need to think of the past.

5. The solution requires you to take responsibility, to live without and to find yourself.

6. Although it is convenient to depend on others, ultimately you need to take responsibility for yourself. In so doing, you will gain your independence and liberty.

7. You must learn to live without your loss and not to try to find a replacement. You need to resist finding a substitute for the loss.

8. A great benefit of renewal is that you find yourself, and you may not be what you used to be, but what you have become as a result of your loss.

CHAPTER NINE

OUT OF THE PIT

The minister was well-known for his passionate views on alcohol consumption. He believed alcohol was the ultimate weapon of the Devil and led people to commit great sins. Year after year, he never tired of preaching to his congregation on the evils of alcoholism. In particular, he hated whisky, and could not understand how anyone could drink the amber liquid. Not content with preaching to adults, he decided that he should warn the young children in his congregation on the evils of whisky. One Sunday, in his children's sermon, he astonished the church by pouring a large glass of whisky. There was silence in the church, he had everyone's total attention and even the central heating stopping making a noise. The minister raised the glass of whisky, pulled a face and shivered in horror and disgust as he placed it in front of him. He then opened a jam jar containing a trapped fly, and held the jar over the whisky so that the fumes from the glass could enter the jar. Slowly the fly stopping buzzing, it started to hold onto the sides of the jar and then it fell into the glass of whisky. The minister then exclaimed :

"This is what whisky can do to a fly. What do you think whisky does to you?"

He then took out of another container a live worm which moved and wriggled as he held it. Slowly, he placed the worm into the glass of whisky. The church watched as the worm furiously wriggled as it fell to the bottom of the glass. A few moments later there was no movement from the worm. The minister pronounced the worm dead and again exclaimed:

"This is what whisky can do to a worm. What do you think whisky does to you?"

This time the minister wanted an answer to his question, but none of the children dared say anything. Finally, his glare fell on wee Ted. The rest of the children breathed a sigh of relief. The whole church was waiting for wee Ted's reply, especially as his father was an established lover of whisky. Wee Ted's reply was a match for the situation :

"Well, Sir, it shows that if you drink whisky you wouldn't be troubled by flies or worms."

-o-0-o-

Observation

An important lesson in life is that we can never take anything for granted. When someone has managed to climb out of the pit of life, everything else should be easier. However, **in some cases, matters can be more difficult when one is out of the pit.** This is often when recovery is taken for granted. It is not unlike the tennis player who has played hard for five sets and is about to win the match when he loses his nerve. Or the migraine sufferer who has managed through the week, but gets a terrible attack whilst relaxing at the weekend. One needs to be continuously vigilant **as life can frequently get worse when one should expect it to get better.** Nevertheless, when one is out of the pit, life should improve if one can keep the momentum going. If one is able to think, plan and work (as one did climbing out of the pit), success should quickly follow.

CASE HISTORIES

CASE ONE

Nigel was a 45 year old and had returned from an arduous business trip to find that his wife had moved out. He was devastated but being a practical man, he concentrated on looking after his children and his work. He slowly climbed out of the pit, developing a great interest in cooking. During the separation, both Nigel and his wife had time to reflect on their 19 years of marriage : there had been some great times and some tough times. They would meet occasionally and each saw great change in the other : some of the changes were predictable, but others were surprising. They recognized that they knew a lot about each other but not everything. This insight was both comforting and fascinating, and they wished that they had spoken to each other more but married life had been too busy and there was always something more pressing and important.

A year later, they happened to meet after a long day and somehow started talking. They ended up having a meal together. Time had been good to them : they had an animated conversation, kept laughing at each other's jokes; and were surprised eventually to find that the restaurant was empty with the staff waiting for them to leave. The next day they telephoned each other, had lunch, had dinner and looked at each other with new love and respect. A few weeks went by and all of their friends felt that a reconciliation was possible. It appeared that the couple had just gone through a mid-life crisis, and now all was being put right before there was anything permanent such as the divorce. Nigel even found himself getting quite excited at the family being together again. A few more idyllic weeks passed. Everything seemed perfect. Nigel was even enjoying doing the housework and wondering how he and his wife would share the jobs if she returned. It was then that Nigel found an old letter from his wife in which she was unkind. He suddenly remembered his feelings of loneliness, anguish and betrayal on his return from his business trip the year before. The great difficulties coping with his work, the children and the house suddenly came rushing back. It was too much. He resolved not to see his wife again. He did not reply to his wife's letters and telephone calls. She never knew why he suddenly had changed.

CASE TWO

Zack was a gifted craftsman and at 35 years had built up a thriving business. Then the 1990's came and business was very bad. Zack lost his business and was without a job on his 40th birthday. However, he was resourceful and took a low paid job painting souvenirs in a local factory. He was happy as he managed to pay the bills and keep his family together. Over the next year, he slowly climbed out of the pit. He regained his self-respect and took great joy in being able to spend a lot of time with his family.

Then the late 1990's arrived and the company he was working for took off. Suddenly, Zack was spending a lot of time at work organising the growing work force and producing new designs and products. He was paid overtime and that was good enough for Zack – it helped pay for the family's holidays. As the months went by, he was not only working longer hours, but he was also taking on more and more responsibility. A frequent comment was that Zack was doing the work of three men. Yet Zack was not being paid as a manager but as a craftsman. Then, after an export drive the company obtained massive export orders. It was obvious that the company could not carry on as before. There was a need for a new manager, someone who could take responsibility, had the respect of the staff and knew the business. Zack was the obvious choice for the job. With great aplomb, a generous executive package was put together – something that Zack could not possibly refuse. Then Zack and his wife were taken out to dinner in a very expensive restaurant.

After dinner, the chairman got up, made a speech, said how much Zack was respected and then asked Zack if he would like to be a partner. It was almost like a marriage proposal. It was late at night and everyone had had too much to drink. Yet, suddenly Zack was sober. He looked around the table and saw smiling, expectant faces. Everyone could only see Zack accepting this very attractive offer. Slowly, Zack put his brandy glass down. He thanked everyone for the kind words and optimism. Then, he looked at his wife. She immediately recognized that Zack could not take the chance that history would repeat itself; he was an older man now and could not bear to go through the turmoil and suffering of the last years again. A moment later he looked at the chairman and declined the offer. As he got up there were protestations, but he just smiled and walked out of the restaurant.

COMMENT

Both of these cases show that **one must not underes-**

timate the trauma caused to the individual in getting out of the pit. Sometimes, the scars can be so deep that the individual develops great fear of being in the pit again. This is sad. The pit of life does not disappear. **As long as we are alive there is a danger that we may fall into the pit.** Yet with these two cases, the individuals were afraid that history would repeat itself and to some extent, they could be right and they both showed that they had learnt some lessons from the pit. However, it is not possible to avoid all the risks of falling into the pit, and one needs to be able to live life despite these risks. It may be that one would choose a slightly different situation than that of the past. But how do you learn to take risks again? How do you live once you have survived the pit? And can one be the same again?

MAJOR FACTORS

The problems of surviving the pit are the same as ordinary individuals have with their lives. As Montaigne said :

"The value of life lies not in the length of days, but in the use you make of them."

The qualities one needs to get out of the pit are quite different to those for building a new life above ground. To climb out of the pit is only to get back to normal, there are no certainties as to what is possible out of the pit. Nevertheless, the resolve and commitment needed to get value out of life are similar to those required to climb out of the pit. Thus, **one can learn from one's experiences, but it is necessary to go through a different process to climb higher.** Although it is reasonable to show caution about the situations that got you into the pit, one must still be able to take risks. It is perhaps important to remember an observation about the turtle :

"The turtle never makes progress until he is prepared to stick his neck out."

Climbing out of the pit should teach us caution, but it should not stop us from sticking our necks out. To make the most of one's life at this stage involves a recognition that one has been wounded and that fear may be present.

1. **Wounded** : As one climbs out of the pit, there is much pain. **Disasters are still close enough for one to feel considerable hurt,** often triggered by everyday happenings. Thus an innocent remark about taxes can trigger anger in someone recently unemployed or bankrupt. Alternatively, an innocent mention of a return to university of a son can pain a friend who has to return to school to resit exams. Somehow, the bleeding seems to be going on and on. Yet, once one has climbed out of the pit, matters are a lot better. **Although there may still be pain and bleeding, it is substantially less than it was in the pit.** One should remind oneself of this fact and rejoice. It would be well to remember William Shakespeare's words :

   "How poor are they that have no patience! What wound did ever heal but by degrees?"

2. **Fear** : In the pit of life, one learns about fear. Fear of one's abilities and fear of the future. Once one has climbed out of the pit, fear continues. But this time it has changed : **there is personal fear of loneliness and fear of forming relationships.** This is perfectly normal. In the pit, one has had to cope with great loss

and accompanying that loss, there is also destruction of self-confidence. When one loses confidence, all of the landmarks in life disappear and one becomes temporarily lost. When one has lost a leg or is scarred in an accident, surely it is not surprising that one has fear of how others may react? Also, if one is without a job or partner, it is reasonable to fear the reactions of acquaintances. Therefore, **fear is both to be expected and is natural if the circumstances of the situation are considered.** For some individuals, it may be the first time that they experience real fear, and it can be overpoweringly frightening. Yet, it is quite a different fear as that of being in the pit. **In the pit, fear is of the present, out of the pit, fear is of the future**. We often fear the future simply because we do not have enough information. When there is sufficient knowledge, fear usually disappears! Franklin Roosevelt in his Inaugural Presidential Address made a pertinent observation :

"The only thing that we have to fear is fear itself."

THE SOLUTION

1. **Healing :** Instead of concentrating on being wounded, you should remember that you are healing. **The pain and bleeding are not part of continuing damage, but are the hopeful signs of time healing.** When you are wounded, a part of you is damaged and lost. To deal with the situation, you need to replace the loss with something that is equally important. Thus, to recover from divorce you may need to find your independence again. Or, to recover from a severe illness, one may need to find love of life again. Love is

a tremendous force as it can produce such positive reactions. St John Chrysostom lived in the fourth century but had some marvellous words to say about love :

"He whom we love and lose is no longer where he was before. He is now wherever we are."

Although "he" in this quotation refers to a person, it does not have to be so. Equally it can be any of the things that put you in the pit, for example a job or a relationship. **The essence is to remember the good of what we had and to know that it will always be part of us.** We, therefore, go into our future lives with a wonderful asset in our memories, and this asset can give us joy and comfort.

2. **Growth** : A child is desperate to measure each half inch of vertical growth. Yet adults seem to be preoccupied with stopping horizontal growth. The truth of the matter is that fat is a minor consideration. **Far more important is your spiritual and intellectual growth.** These are not measured in inches but in what you can suffer and accomplish. In some instances, you might have everything going your way and success is guaranteed. However, what makes you special is if you can turn disaster into triumph. To be able to play a hand with bad cards and win is a testament of your strength and growth. The pit of life can be seen as the worst thing possible. Alternatively it can be regarded as a learning experience. It is like digging over the garden in the winter, it is hard work and the rewards do not come until the following year. If there is to be good growth, the ground has to be prepared well. **If you can climb out of the pit of life, you have prepared the ground for personal**

growth. It will not be easy or straightforward, but the potential will be there – a golden opportunity is within your grasp.

THE NEXT PIT

Once one has climbed out of the pit of life, there is the temptation to think that all will be well for the rest of one's life. If this were so, life would be too easy. The reality is that we live a life in which there are lots of pits in the ground. **With a normal life, we shall probably fall into 3–4 pits during our lifetime.** Some people will not be able to get out of their first. Others will find the first few easy, but remain in the third. At certain times of life, it is easier to fall into a pit, for example at major life changes such as adolescence, mid-life, menopause or retirement. The real lesson is that **once one has climbed out of the pit, it is now possible to fall into another!** Confucius has said :
"Our greatest glory is not in never falling, but in rising every time we fall."
The pit of life is part of life. The more active you are, the more likely you are to fall into the pit. However, the pit should not be feared. By teaching ourselves to climb out, whatever our age, we learn more about ourselves and those around us. Like the rest of life, the pit is a great teacher, **and climbing out of the pit is a valuable life experience although it never feels so at the time!**

SUMMARY

1. Life can be more difficult once you have climbed out

of a pit of life, especially if you start to take life for granted again.

2. Much effort is required to climb out of the pit and the individual may not want ever to repeat the experience. Although you may not want history to repeat itself, you must still be able to take some risks.

3. The process to get out of the pit is quite different to that for rebuilding a life above ground. Yet, the resolve and commitment are the same and can bring success out of the pit.

4. To be able to climb higher, one needs to recognize that one is wounded and has great fear.

5. Although one feels great pain and bleeding, it is substantially less than it was in the pit.

6. Fear of loneliness and forming relationships is perfectly normal. It results from a lack of self-confidence.

7. You need to recognize that the pain and bleeding are due to the healing process; your experience of loss can be an asset and will be in your memory forever; you will need to grow spiritually and intellectually.

8. You may find yourself in 3–4 pits in a normal life-span. The pit is a great teacher, and climbing out of the pit is a valuable life experience although it may not feel so at the time!

CHAPTER TEN

HAPPINESS

The dinner party was a great success. The food was superb, the wine quite excellent and the conversation had been particularly stimulating. At this point, one of the guests commented :

"This is my idea of happiness : wonderful food, wine and company!"

His remark received several nods of agreement but then an attractive woman said :

"Oh no. This is not real happiness because it is too ordinary. I have to have excitement to be happy. Earlier this year, I went on a week's holiday to Rome and met a wonderful man. He was completely adorable and he did everything for me. He was a man who knew how to entertain and I had the holiday of a lifetime!" She then went on to add that she had not been in touch with this man since – it was just a wonderful holiday romance.

The next guest had a quite different story :

"I can only be happy if I have accomplished something after physical effort. The happiest moments of my life are when I reach the tops of mountains. Nothing else compares with that total feeling of contentment after one has spent the last six hours climbing to the top. It just cannot be beaten."

This guest had always had difficulty expressing his feelings to others. He liked to be totally in control and spent most of his weekends climbing.

His remarks were quickly followed by those of a

retired bank manager :

"No, no. All of this physical activity is bad for you. It destroys your knees and you will have severe arthritis when you reach my age. Happiness is very simple. It is a hot summer's day when you have had a good lunch and a couple of pints in the local public house, and then spend the afternoon dozing watching the cricket on the village green!!"

Everyone was able to understand the reasons for all of the comments, especially as each of the situations of happiness was such a reflection of the character of the particular individual. However, the next comment was surprising. It came from Brian, a middle-aged man who never demonstrated much emotion. He slowly told of his last visit to his son and daughter-in-law. As was his way, he had invited everyone out for a meal. It was a good evening and Brian had to go to the toilet at the end of the dinner. When he returned to the table, the others had left and were waiting for him in the foyer. He could see his son was holding his jacket, so as he passed the table he picked up the bill. His son was 33 years old but Brian had always paid the dinner bills; it was a sort of family tradition. When he found the others, he put on his jacket and reached for his wallet. Just then, his son took the bill and said:

"No, Dad. I pay the bills from now on."

-o-O-o-

Observation

Happiness means different things to different people. For many, happiness is reminiscing pleasurable events

112

in the past, such as dinner parties or climbing mountains. However, **total happiness cannot be planned.** The right environment can be created, but there cannot be any guarantee that total happiness will result. **Happiness is best when it surprises.** Like Brian who had always expected to pay the bill, but totally unpredictably his son pays. He is surprised by total happiness. But more than this, this event is a first and so unique. Unplanned, it also demonstrates to Brian that his son has become responsible. **People do not find total happiness, total happiness finds people.** Like the beautiful sunset or silent dawn, it is an unpredictable gift of life.

MAJOR FACTORS

There is far more written about depression than there is about happiness. It is almost as sex was in the last century : no-one told you much about it and everyone was supposed to be instinctively good at it. The truth is **if one can understand more of how and why one becomes happy, life dramatically improves.**

1. **Definition** : There are many words to express happiness and general use of these words have made the situation more confusing. Thus, "happy" may mean "joy" or "total elation", and everyone understands the intense feelings of "I was so happy on my wedding day." However, "happy" may also mean "convinced" and can be used in a detective story as "Were you happy that the man was dead?" Although this may be appropriate for a woman with a violet husband, it is usually addressed to the doctor

attending the scene of the crime. **My use of the word happiness in this book is as follows :-**

a) several words and phrases are similar to happiness such as feeling good, satisfied or pleased.

b) happiness or the words in (a) may be subdivided into : joy and elation, followed by excitement and then contentment. The same effect may be obtained by adding prefixes such as great/some/little to words in a). Therefore, great happiness (satisfaction or pleasure) is similar to joy or elation; and little happiness (satisfaction or pleasure) is similar to contentment.

It is immediately obvious that in the story at the start of this chapter, the guests at the dinner party were speaking of different subdivisions of happiness. The comments in the observation after the story are of total happiness – the peak, the very best. Thus, happiness is a reflection of the degree of satisfaction that a person has of his/her life, and total happiness is the very highest satisfaction.

2. **Unhappiness** : It is worth considering the concept of unhappiness. What is clear is **unhappiness is not entirely the opposite of happiness.** At first, this may appear surprising, but when people are questioned about happiness and unhappiness, they seem to experience both together in many instances. Thus a couple may be very happy (as measured by frequency of sexual intercourse), but at the same time be very unhappy (as judged by the number of

114

arguments). Love also is interesting as it manifests both happiness and unhappiness. At the start of the relationship, it is very positive; but later, negative feelings become common. Indeed, as people know more about each other, there is more to disagree about. Thus, **happiness and unhappiness can be independent emotions, so both may be present at the same time.** Yet, the absence of unhappiness can mean happiness, especially if someone else is suffering.

"Uneasy lies the head that mixed hot chili, horse-radish and ice-cream at dinner."

This statement can make you happy that you are not going through the unhappiness. Therefore **we also feel happy that we do not have others' misfortune.**

3. Personal Factors :

a) outlook

An individual's outlook is perhaps the greatest factor in happiness. **Some people are hardly ever happy whilst others are hardly ever unhappy.** Dr Samuel Johnson recognized the importance of a happy outlook:

"It is worth a thousand pounds a year to have the habit of looking on the bright side of things."

With inflation, this would be equivalent to fifty thousand pounds per year today.

b) age

Studies of happiness have shown that young people get more happiness out of leisure activities; middle-aged individuals are more pre-occupied with work; and the elderly are particularly concerned with health. **Age is a major factor in determining the area one gets most happiness.** This is not surprising as our energy and body's capabilities can vary dramatically with age. As Mark Twain said :

"Life would be infinitely happier if we could only be born at the age of eighty and gradually approach eighteen."

c) **sex and marriage**

Large surveys of the population have found that on the whole women tend to be happier than men. The most unhappy tend to be young, single men. Married people are more happy on average than those unmarried, widowed or divorced. Unmarried men are less happy than unmarried women, and men get more out of marriage than women. Couples living together are usually not as happy as those married, but are more happy than those single. Thus **women are the happier sex and men get most out of marriage.** Perhaps there is more truth in the story of a daughter asking her mother what makes a marriage successful and getting the following reply :

"I think that you had better ask your father. After all, he made a more successful marriage than I did."

d) **prosperity**

International studies have shown that there is little difference in happiness between rich and poor countries. This is probably because within each country, a person's relative prosperity to others is the same. Nevertheless, **happiness tends to be**

less as prosperity increases, possibly because individuals have more options rather than being forced to make the best of their circumstances. Lee Segall describes the position well :

"It's possible to own too much. A man with one watch knows what time it is; a man with two watches is never quite sure."

4. **Amount** : When a large sample of people are asked about their happiness, there is a mixed response. On a percentage scale, 22% say that they are completely satisfied, 1% are completely dissatisfied and 77% are in between. However, overall 88% are satisfied to some extent. This figure is remarkably high and may just reflect that people do not like to admit to being unhappy. Perhaps, another survey is more revealing as it found that 50% of adults had symptoms of unhappiness; but 71% of them did nothing, 12% talked to friends and only 17% saw a doctor. It appears that many people look upon unhappiness as part of life. **All of the available studies show that only a minority of the population are happy at any time.** Sydney Smith has made a suggestion on why there is so much happiness :

"Why destroy present happiness by distant misery, which may never come at all, or you may never live to see it? For every substantial grief has twenty shadows and most of these shadows are of your own making."

He may be quite right and that **WE IMAGINE problems that interfere with our happiness.**

THE SOLUTION

In the Declaration of Independence, part of the constitution of the United States of America, is the following statement:-

> "We hold these truths to be self-evident – that all men are created equal; that they are endowed by their Creator with certain unalienable rights; that among these are life, liberty, **and the pursuit of happiness.**"

You should recognize that this statement does not promise happiness for free people, simply that they may be able to pursue happiness. To climb out of the pit of life is to do well. Yet, to climb higher and achieve happiness is much more difficult. It involves a different outlook in which **you need to examine your personal life, relationships and environment.**

1. **Personal life** : In the pursuit of happiness, it is important to examine your needs. **Many people refuse to be happy if they are ill, unemployed or without money.** This is sad. These situations do not affect an individual's capacity to be happy. **No matter what the circumstances, everyone has the same potential to be happy each day.** If you refuse to be happy, an opportunity is lost. It is worth remembering John Mill's statement :

> "I have learnt to seek my happiness by limiting my desires, rather than in attempting to satisfy them."

For many, happiness is in a fantasy world which cannot be achieved. It is much better to cope with the reality of your existence. Apart from changing your desires, you can reinforce positive thoughts. This can be done by simply repeating simple statements to oneself each day such as :

"I am happy. This is a good day" or "Each day, in every way, I am better."
Similarly, a motivating song or a short film can make you a lot happier. **You should say things to yourself and allow songs or films to make you happier each day.** Comparison of your situation with others less fortunate is also a great help, and there is much in being able to "count your blessings!". Happiness requires a positive attempt, but the effects can be long-lasting, not only on your outlook but also on your health.

2. **Relationships** : How you feel depends on your relationships. There are special relationships such as in marriage or family which need a lot of attention. For these, you need patience and a willingness, on both sides, to improve the quality of the relationship. However, **it is often in the friends you choose that there are most problems.** As Delille said :
    "Chance makes our parents, but choice makes our friends."
Friends are usually of two types : rewarding and non-rewarding. Some people are a joy to be with, their company stimulates and excites and you feel better after the meeting. Whereas, non-rewarding friends are like a black hole which drains your energy as these friends moan and complain about everything. **The secret is to have more rewarding friends in your life and only be with non-rewarding friends when you are strong.** It can also affect you as you slowly become like your friends so it makes great sense to choose friends wisely.

3. **Environment** : In my book, "Unwind! Understand and

119

Control Life, Be Better!!" (Dodona Books, 1991, reprinted 1994), I said **stress is a process in which the resources of the person are matched against the demands of the environment.** Stress is perhaps the greatest destroyer of happiness, and you need to recognize when it is present. Work is very important in our lives, and it is sad that many do not appreciate its importance until they are made unemployed. The essence is to start to enjoy work, even if it is only the coffee. **When you spend so much of your life at work, you need to make it pleasurable.** Leisure time is also not for wasting. Like work, how you spend your leisure provides part of your status and reinforces your life in the community. At the same time, **your leisure must allow you to relax and unwind from your work.** You must make time to "fester" – even if it is just sitting in front of the television and falling asleep. Sleep is nature's healer and must not be resisted. Some of the happiest creatures around us are our pets and they do not resist sleeping, so learn from them.

CONCLUSION

Happiness is an ideal that everyone wants, but money or education cannot guarantee. Dorothy Rowe in her book "Wanting Everything. The Art of Happiness" (Harper Collins, 1991) makes an intelligent observation on happiness :

"We can go on as we always have, not thinking clearly, relying on our hope that somehow, by some magical means, it will all come right in the end. Or we can take what we have and recycle or rearrange it

120

with careful, clear thought and create, out of what we have already got, all that we want."

This is the essence. **It is nearly always possible to have total happiness out of what you already have.** There is no need to live in the past or in the future. As has been said :

"The past is a cashed cheque, the future is an IOU, the only real money is the present."

Happiness is now.

SUMMARY

1. Total happiness cannot be planned and is usually a surprise. Total happiness finds people rather than people finding it.

2. There are many words for happiness and it is important to have a good definition. Happiness is a reflection of the degree of satisfaction that a person has of his/her life.

3. Unhappiness is not entirely the opposite of happiness. Both are independent emotions and can be present at the same time.

4. Happiness is influenced by several personal factors such as outlook, sex, age, if married and prosperity.

5. Only a minority of the population are happy at any one time, and there may be an acceptance that unhappiness is part of life.

6. The pursuit of happiness is a liberty, yet many people

refuse to be happy because of their personal circumstances.

7. One secret is to have friends who make you feel better rather than those who absorb your energy.

8. Stress in your environment is a destroyer of happiness, and you must try to create work and leisure situations that reinforce happiness.

9. It is possible to gain total happiness out of what you already have by using clear thinking and creativity.

CHAPTER ELEVEN

CONCLUSION

It is our destiny that on average each of us shall fall into the pit 3–4 times in a lifetime. The longer we live and the more active our lives, the more we will find ourselves in the pit of life. **The pit of life (Chapter One) is about many situations in which we face a serious loss : death of a loved one, the end of a relationship, severe illness, financial ruin, a severe accident, betrayal, public humiliation, loss of a job, or an enforced change of life.** In the past, many books have concentrated on bereavement as this loss is the greatest. This book recognizes that the same process occurs in many other circumstances, provided that the individual perceives that there was a great loss.

An understanding of this process will allow the individual to climb out of the pit quicker. The ladder (Chapter Two) describes the important stages of the process. Depending on the person and the situation, each stage of the ladder may have a different order and may be more or less severe. Nevertheless **everyone usually goes through the seven stages of the ladder : lifeless, anger, denial, disgrace, endeavour and renewal.** Each stage has been discussed in a separate chapter and also for each stage, solutions are offered on the important points to recognize and overcome. For many individuals, there is the perception that their loss and circumstances are unique and cannot be appreciated by anyone else. This is untrue. It is similar to the many circumstances under which one may cut a finger (some situations can be bizarre), however the process of the body healing after the cut is the same. Thus **although the circumstances of a serious loss may be unique, the process of the body healing after the loss is the same.**

Being **lifeless** (Chapter Three) is a response to one's loss and can be complete, with some remaining in this stage for the rest of their lives. Others may depend on time, luck or chance to progress to the next stage. The solution is to behave as though one is alive and start to satisfy your physical and emotional needs. **Anger** (Chapter Four) is complex and there are five main types of anger so one needs to identify what types are appropriate to one's situation. The solution then involves knowledge and in particular the 3D's blocking techniques to deal effectively with anger. **Denial** (Chapter Five) is necessary as the loss is often too much for the person to cope with. Although denial gains valuable time, to progress one must accept the truth. **Disgrace** (Chapter Six) is the public's perception of one's loss. The solution depends on recognizing the importance of knowledge, time and acceptance. **Endeavour** (Chapter Seven) requires the individual to start to work and really try hard again. The solution involves an understanding of one's personal and social situation. **Renewal** (Chapter Eight) is a testament of one's ability to deal with being put into the pit of life. Important factors to recognize in renewal are a dependence on others, the need to find a replacement for the loss and to resist thinking of the past.

Life can be more difficult once one has climbed **out of**

the pit (Chapter Nine), as the qualities needed to climb out of the pit are different to those required to build above ground. The solution is in the healing process and growth. Most importantly, is one's concept of **happiness** (Chapter Ten). Total happiness finds people rather than people finding it. Sadly, only a minority of the population are happy at any one time. **A secret is recognizing that it is possible to have total happiness out of what you already have.**

This book is about living. It deals with the situations when one is put in the pit of life, and offers solutions for climbing out of the pit. But more than this, **there are opportunities for growth and for the individual to be renewed.** Once one has experienced such a process, one becomes stronger and total happiness is possible. Sadly this is not an end and there may be another pit ahead. The pit of life is not a once in a lifetime experience. **One needs to learn that the pit is simply a part of life which must be endured, and then one can progress to greater heights.**

Unwind!
Understand and control life,
be better!!

(ISBN 0-9511090-2-2)

by Dr Darrel Ho-Yen

Many individuals are having great difficulties in living in a modern society. The stress on these people may produce ill health. This book shows that stress can be reduced by the acquisition of skills. **This book was first published in 1991 and reprinted in 1994.**

The skill of unwinding (EMBME) is explained in great detail, and has benefits of physical and mental relaxation. **Both well and ill individuals would benefit from this skill.**

With the ability to unwind, you can start to develop the skill to understand your life and identify your problems. The skill to control your life is achieved by good use of time, use of the reward/effort ratio and good decision-making. **With the acquisition of these skills, you have the opportunity for self-improvement, happiness and to be better.**

Obtainable from : Dodona Books

BETTER RECOVERY FROM VIRAL ILLNESSES

(ISBN 0-9511090-3-0)

by Dr Darrel Ho-Yen

The first edition of this book was the first book published (April 1985) on Post Viral Fatigue Syndrome (myalgic encephalo-myelitis, Royal Free Disease, Chronic Fatigue Syndrome). The second edition was published in 1987; and this **third edition** was published in 1993 (and reprinted in 1994).

Over the years the author has given many lectures throughout Britain and this book contains 37 illustrations in 240 pages. **The lay-out is designed for those with a limited concentration span.**

Unlike other books, this book provides a five step plan for better recovery which has been used by very many patients. This book is a product of the collective experiences and recovery of these patients. **It provides the information and motivation for the patient to recover.**

Obtainable from : Dodona Books

ISBN 0-9511090-4-9

Publishers and distributors:
Dodona Books
The Old Schoolhouse
Kirkhill
Inverness
IV5 7PE